Second Workshop on Understanding Implicit and Underspecified Language (UNIMPLICIT 2022)

Online
15 June 2022

ISBN: 978-1-7138-5644-3

Printed from e-media with permission by:

Curran Associates, Inc.
57 Morehouse Lane
Red Hook, NY 12571

CURRAN ASSOCIATES INC. proceedings.com

Some format issues inherent in the e-media version may also appear in this print version.

Association for Computational Linguistics
209 N. Eighth Street
Stroudsburg, Pennsylvania 18360

Phone: 1-570-476-8006
Fax: 1-570-476-0860

acl@aclweb.org

Additional copies of this publication are available from:

Curran Associates, Inc.
57 Morehouse Lane
Red Hook, NY 12571 USA
Phone: 845-758-0400
Fax: 845-758-2633
Email: curran@proceedings.com
Web: www.proceedings.com

UnImplicit 2022

The Second Workshop on Understanding Implicit and Underspecified Language

Proceedings of the Workshop

July 15, 2022

The UnImplicit organizers gratefully acknowledge the support from the following sponsors.

Gold

Meta

Order copies of this and other ACL proceedings from:

Association for Computational Linguistics (ACL)
209 N. Eighth Street
Stroudsburg, PA 18360
USA
Tel: +1-570-476-8006
Fax: +1-570-476-0860
acl@aclweb.org

Introduction

Welcome to UnImplicit: The Second Workshop on Understanding Implicit and Underspecified Language. The focus of this workshop is on implicit and underspecified phenomena in language, which pose serious challenges to standard natural language processing models as they often require incorporating greater context, using symbolic inference and common-sense reasoning, or more generally, going beyond strictly lexical and compositional meaning constructs. This challenge spans all phases of the NLP model's life cycle: from collecting and annotating relevant data, through devising computational methods for modeling such phenomena, to evaluating and designing proper evaluation metrics.
In this workshop, our goal is to bring together theoreticians and practitioners from the entire NLP cycle, from annotation and benchmarking to modeling and applications, and to provide an umbrella for the development, discussion and standardization of the study of understanding implicit and underspecified language.
In total, we received 11 submissions (6 of which non-archival), out of which 10 were accepted and 1 was withdrawn. All accepted submissions are presented as posters and two works are additionally presented in an oral presentation. The workshop also includes three invited talks on topics related to implicit language. The program committee consisted of 22 researchers, who we'd like to thank for providing helpful and constructive reviews on the papers. We'd also like to thank all authors for their submissions and interest in our workshop.

Valentina, Daniel and Talita

Organizing Committee

Organizers

Talita Anthonio, Stuttgart University
Valentina Pyatkin, Bar-Ilan University
Daniel Fried, Meta AI and University of Washington

Advisory Committee

Michael Roth, Stuttgart University
Reut Tsarfaty, Bar-Ilan University and AI2
Yoav Goldberg, Bar-Ilan University and AI2

Program Committee

Program Committee

Maria Becker, University of Heidelberg
Eunsol Choi, UT Austin
Vera Demberg, Saarland University
Yanai Elazar, Bar-Ilan University
Katrin Erk, UT Austin
Dan Goldwasser, Purdue University
Daniel Hershcovich, University of Copenhagen
Jennifer Hu, MIT
Lucy Li, UC Berkeley
Philippe Muller, University Paul Sabatier
Aida Nematzadeh, DeepMind
Sebastian Pado, University of Stuttgart
Roma Patel, Brown University
Massimo Poesio, Queen Mary University of London
Chris Potts, Stanford University
Vered Shwartz, University of British Columbia
Elias Stengel-Eskin, Johns Hopkins University
Elior Sulem, University of Pennsylvania
Tiago Torrent, Federal University of Juiz de Fora
Nicholas Tomlin, UC Berkeley
Sara Tonelli, Fondazione Bruno Kessler
Luke Zettlemoyer, University of Washington

Invited Speakers

Judith Degen, Stanford University, USA
Michael Franke, University of Tübingen, Germany
Nathan Schneider, Georgetown University, USA

Table of Contents

Program

Friday, July 15, 2022

08:30 - 08:45	*Welcome + Opening Remarks*
08:45 - 09:30	*Invited Talk 1*
10:00 - 10:30	*Break*
10:30 - 11:00	*Session A*
	Pre-trained Language Models' Interpretation of Evaluativity Implicature: Evidence from Gradable Adjectives Usage in Context Yan Cong
	Searching for PETs: Using Distributional and Sentiment-Based Methods to Find Potentially Euphemistic Terms Patrick Lee, Martha Gavidia, Anna Feldman and Jing Peng
11:00 - 12:00	*Poster*
12:00 - 13:30	*Lunch*
13:30 - 14:15	*Session B*
14:15 - 15:00	*Invited Talk 2*
15:00 - 15:30	*Break*
15:30 - 16:15	*Invited Talk 3*
16:15 - 16:45	*Session C*
16:45 - 17:00	*Closing Remarks*

Pre-trained Language Models' Interpretation of Evaluativity Implicature: Evidence from Gradable Adjectives Usage in Context

Yan Cong
yancong222@gmail.com

Abstract

By saying *Maria is tall*, a human speaker typically implies that Maria is *evaluatively* tall from the speaker's perspective. However, by using a different construction *Maria is taller than Sophie*, we cannot infer from Maria and Sophie's relative heights that Maria is evaluatively tall because it is possible for Maria to be taller than Sophie in a context in which they both count as short. Can pre-trained language models (LMs) "understand" evaulativity (EVAL) inference? To what extent can they discern the EVAL salience of different constructions in a conversation? Will it help LMs' implicitness performance if we give LMs a persona such as chill, social, and pragmatically skilled? Our study provides an approach to probing LMs' interpretation of EVAL inference by incorporating insights from experimental pragmatics and sociolinguistics. We find that with the appropriate prompt, LMs can succeed in *some* pragmatic level language understanding tasks. Our study suggests that socio-pragmatics methodology can shed light on the challenging questions in NLP.

1 Introduction

This paper concerns pre-trained Language Models' (LMs) interpretation of context-specific implicit elements on the pragmatic level of language understanding. Probing LMs' competence in implicitness is challenging due to the lack of surface representation. In this paper, we attempt to tease apart exactly what LMs "know" about pragmatics through a case study of gradable adjectives such as *tall*. We draw insights from experimental pragmatics and sociolinguistics, and implement them in probing two types of transformer LMs: the traditional auto-regressive GPT-3 (Brown et al., 2020) and the encoder-decoder model Macaw (Tafjord and Clark, 2021). Our findings show that the extent to which LMs are sensitive to implicitness depends on adjective properties (class, polarity, construction), prompt setting (the speaker is predefined as chill or nerdy), and transformers' architecture (decoder-transformer such as GPT-3, encoder-decoder transformer like Macaw).

By uttering a positive construction (henceforth POS) *Alex is tall*, conversational participants simultaneously extract two kinds of meaning: its descriptive literal meaning about the state of the world - Alex's height is above a particular threshold (Cresswell, 1976; von Stechow, 1984; Bierwisch, 1989); its socio-indexical meaning which implicitly reveals about the speakers themselves - Alex is tall from the speaker's perspective, namely the speaker *implies* that Alex is *evaluatively* tall (Bierwisch, 1989; Rett, 2008a,b). By contrast, when uttering an equative construction (henceforth EQ) like *Alex is as tall as Arthur*, or a comparative construction (henceforth COMP) such as *Alex is taller than Arthur*, there is no such salient *evaluative* reading because it's likely that Alex is as tall as or taller than Arthur in a context where (the speaker thinks) they are both short. A construction is evaluative if and only if it contextually entails its POS counterpart (Bierwisch, 1989; Brasoveanu and Rett, 2018). This is called the Bierwisch Test: by using *Alex is tall* (POS), the speaker implies that Alex is *evaluatively* tall; while by using *Alex is as tall as Arthur* (EQ) or *Alex is taller than Arthur* (COMP), the speaker is not implying that Alex is *evaluatively* tall - hence the linguistic generalization: using POS gives rise to evaluativity (henceforth EVAL) implicatures, whereas using EQ or COMP does not. We make all code and test data available for additional testing [1]

EVAL is a central member of the class of context-sensitive phenomena. It arises as a pragmatic inference - a conversational implicature (Rett, 2015, 2019; Bumford and Rett, 2020). Our paper proposes LMs examination schemes through a case study on EVAL implicature. Our study is built up

[1] https://github.com/yancong222/Unimplicit

Proceedings of the Second Workshop on Understanding Implicit and Underspecified Language, pages 1 - 7
July 15, 2022

on Brasoveanu and Rett (2018), which adopts the Bierwisch Test to test for the the presence of EVAL inference in different gradable adjectives. Their experimental pragmatics findings show a comprehensive picture about EVAL implicature (human judgment data, N=95): humans think that EVAL implicature is highly dependent on *context* which is shaped by the speaker's usage of adjective class (relative, e.g. *heavy*, absolute, e.g. *full*), adjective polarity (positive: *tall*, negative: its antonym *short*), and construction (POS, EQ, COMP). Their experiment result (Table2) showed that regarding adjective polarity, there is no clear difference in EVAL between positive and negative adjectives within either the relative or the absolute class. Regarding construction, POS is clearly the most evaluative. Regarding adjective class, the relative adjective class is less evaluative than the absolute in POS, but more evaluative than the absolute in EQ, and exhibit the same EVAL as the absolute in COMP. Our LMs investigation implemented Brasoveanu and Rett (2018)'s dataset to examine the extent to which LMs align with humans.

Throughout Brasoveanu and Rett (2018)'s dataset, only one template prompt was used. Thus, as a sanity check, we varied the prompt by adding two distinct personality illustration to the input. Another motivation of taking prompt design to be an independent variable is that an utterance's socio-indexing meaning and its speaker's personality traits are intertwined: it reveals about the speakers' demographic background and ideological orientation (Labov, 2006; Silverstein, 2003; Eckert, 2008; Podesva, 2011). We designed the prompt text based on *speaker persona*: a social construct shown to be central to social meaning across various domains of language (Eckert, 2008; Podesva, 2011). We argue that the construct of persona is relevant to LMs examination because: i) it's well-known and readily available for perceiving social identity in human interaction; ii) it's been shown to shape human language processing at different levels (Niedzielski, 1999; Strand, 1999; Casasanto, 2008; Choe et al., 2019); iii) personae tend to be indexed by a variety of (non-)linguistic signs, including a mere textual description of the persona at stake (D'onofrio, 2018), making them easy to invoke in LMs experiment set up.

Specifically, our incorporation of *persona* in the prompt design is inspired by Beltrama and Schwarz (2021). They find that to compute the standard of precision required to interpret numeral expressions, human comprehenders reason about the speaker's social identity, particularly about the persona they embody. An utterance produced by a nerdy speaker is associated with higher standard of precision, hence the tendency to interpreting the literal meaning but not necessarily the socio-indexing pragmatic implicit meaning, compared to the same utterance in the same context uttered by a chill speaker. Our experiments on LMs take two opposite sets of characters: a persona interpreting utterance with its literal meaning (Nerd), and a persona embodying laid-backness and pragmatic skillfulness (Chill). We framed these two persona in the prompt text, and examined if this could help LMs "understand" EVAL implicatures across various adjectives. We found that the answer depends on adjective properties and LMs' types.

A lot of attention has been paid to increase LMs' general transparency (Ettinger, 2020; Rogers et al., 2020), among which studies on LMs' interpretation of implicitness mostly focus on scalar implicature or presupposition (Schuster et al., 2020; Jeretic et al., 2020; Pandia et al., 2021). To our knowledge, no studies in this line have been done on gradable adjectives' EVAL implicature, although EVAL and gradability are classic topics in context sensitivity. This is probably because these phenomena are cognitively too subtle to spot, hence hard to quantify under a LMs framework.

Against this background, our goal is to examine the extent to which pre-trained LMs can "understand" implicit EVAL implicatures. We hypothesized that if pre-trained LMs are cognitively plausible, their performance should align with the human data in Brasoveanu and Rett (2018) and Beltrama and Schwarz (2021), namely: i) there should be no EVAL difference regarding adjective polarity, ii) LMs should predict POS constructions to be the most evaluative, iii) whether LMs consider the relative adjectives to be more or less evaluative than the absolute adjectives depends on construction type, iv) LMs should (at least) show a trend that the chill-persona prompt helps LMs' understanding of implicatures, relative to the nerdy-persona prompt.

2 Experiments

We designed our tests in the form of completion tasks, so as to test the pre-trained LMs in their most natural setting, without interference from fine-tuning. We presented all the tasks in a conversation format involving agent(s), meaning LMs are expected to interpret the utterance with some conversational level of language understanding. We focus on two distinct types of transformers (Table1): Macaw (Tafjord and Clark, 2021), which is more recent (built on top of T5 Raffel et al. (2020)), and GPT-3 (Brown et al., 2020). We used the 32 gradable antonym pairs (16 relative adjectives and 16 absolute adjectives) in Brasoveanu and Rett (2018), because it's already quantitatively justified by human judgments. Each antonym pair was syntactically framed in 3 distinct types of constructions: POS, EQ and COMP. This gave us 32 (adjectives) x 3 (constructions) = 96 strings of sequence.

Model	n_{params}	n_{layers}
Macaw-large (c.f. T5)	770M	24
GPT-3/InstructGPT	175B	96

Table 1: (pre-trained LMs) Model cards

Input representation We adapted Brasoveanu and Rett (2018)'s conversational prompt template involving multiple agents. LMs were presented with deductions a Police Chief (*agent*1) makes based on one-sentence utterance reports from his Detective (*agent*2) - *The Detective reported to the Police Chief: "Maria is as short as Sophie." What can the Chief conclude from this?*. LMs completed the prompt with a fixed max-length of sequence (*max_tokens*=100). We preset the penalty and the presence coefficients as 0.6, which were reasonable values if the aim is to just reduce repetitive samples (Brown et al., 2020). All the stimuli had the same format, the only strings that changed were the Detective's quoted report (underlined), which was replaced by different adjectival constructions.

In terms of prompt template, there were 3 variations: in addition to the Detective report, we adopted the Nerd versus Chill persona idea proposed and quantitatively justified by Beltrama and Schwarz (2021) (N=240). Their human data showed that Arthur, who is overwhelmingly seen as embodying social qualities indicative of nerd, is consistently associated with a geeky stereotype and tend to be insensitive to pragmatic cues, whereas Alex is ascribed attributes such as chill and a sociable personality, and he is pragmatically savvy. LMs were prompted with (1) Nerd persona: *Arthur is clever, smart, quiet, awkward, nerdy, shy and geeky. What does he mean by saying "Maria is tall"?* (2) Chill persona: *Alex is chill, laid-back, relaxed, easy, cool, friendly, and outgoing. What doe he imply by saying "Maria is tall"?*. All the adjectives used in the two persona prompts are from Beltrama and Schwarz (2021)'s collection of human responses to nerdy/chill stereotypes. All the stimuli had the same format, the only strings that changed were the speaker's (Alex or Arthur) quoted statement (underlined), which was replaced with various target adjectival constructions. The prompt examples are given in Table 3.

Measurement Inspired by the Bierwisch Test (Bierwisch, 1989), we hypothesized that a construction is evaluative if and only if it contextually entails its POS counterpart. We therefore used GPT-3 similarity embedding model *text-similarity-babbage-001* to embed document as a single vector (Brown et al., 2020). We deployed the model to both LMs' responses and the target utterance (the testing adjectival construction's POS counterpart). We then calculated the cosine distance of the two vectors. The similarity score is calculated only between LMs' own response and the target utterance (see Table 3 for examples).

Adopting Iter et al. (2018)'s semantic similarity metrics, where larger amounts of concept overlap between two text segments is interpreted as more similar, we computed the cosine similarity as a proxy to the measurement of the concept overlap between LMs' response and the target inference. We took that to be how much implicit meaning LMs can pick up in the conversation. For example, in the Detective setting with EQ in the Detective's quoted report "*Maria is as short as Sophie*", the target utterance is its POS counterpart *Maria is short*. Suppose LMs "understand" the EVAL implicature, LMs should draw a POS evaluative inference from EQ. This is reflected in the similarity: LMs' response is predicted to be similar to the target utterance if LMs makes the appropriate pragmatic inference.

3 Results and Discussion

With respect to **polarity** (Fig.1), the results align with human data. There is no statistically significant difference in EVAL between positive and negative adjectives within either the relative adjective class or the absolute adjective class. Regarding **constructions** (Fig.2), consistent with humans, the POS construction shows the highest similarity to the target inference: POS is the most evaluative across different LMs and adjective types. Regarding **LMs** in Fig.2, GPT-3 is more human-like than Macaw regarding construction sensitivity. GPT-3's output shows that using POS implies EVAL, using EQ is less likely to imply EVAL, and using COMP is the least likely to imply EVAL. By contrast, Macaw's output response to different constructions is not as stable: a lot of variance is found especially in Macaw - Nerdy interpreting EQ and COMP. Relative to GPT-3, Macaw is more sensitive to input instructions: with Chill personality, Macaw's "endorsement" of POS being evaluative gets significantly improved; whereas given nerdy personality (Macaw - Nerdy) or without any explicit identity, just interpreting Detective's report (Macaw - Detective), Macaw's sensitivity to constructions is not as salient. On the other hand, regardless of personality setup, GPT-3 showed similar patterns to different constructions.

With respect to **adjective class**: for POS (Fig.3 left), except for Macaw - Detective which considers relative adjectives to be *slightly* more evaluative than the absolute, LMs' output shows that the relative adjective class is less evaluative than the absolute adjective class. This effect is statistically significant for Macaw - Nerdy. Surprisingly, for both EQ (Fig.3 middle) and COMP (Fig.3 right), LMs still output representations suggesting that the relative adjectives are less evaluative than the absolute adjectives, especially for Macaw in which statistical significance was found. An exception was found in GPT - Detective in COMP, which judges relative as more evaluative than the absolute. GPT-3 did not seem to outperform Macaw, although t-test showed that GPT-3 did not *significantly* interpret absolute adjectives to be more evaluative than relative adjectives. In almost all of the cases, LMs indiscriminately "understood" absolute adjectives to be more evaluative than relative adjectives. Overall their interpretation of EVAL implicatures is not sensitive to construction.

Introducing socio-pragmatic frameworks in LMs evaluation loop, we adopted theory-driven hypothesis and cognitively justified datasets to analyze LMs' interpretation of EVAL implicature across adjective types. We found that LMs align with human data in that both suggest that polarity does not influence EVAL, and both considered POS to be the most evaluative across all adjective types, but deviant from linguistic theory and human cognition, most LMs' output suggests that the relative adjectives are *less* evaluative than the absolute across constructions. The persona setting helped *some* LMs "understand" implicitness. We provide an attempt to tackle challenging NLP questions using validated socio-pragmatic paradigms.

4 Limitation and Future studies

In this paper, we investigated the extent to which pre-trained transformer LMs (GPT-3 and Macaw) capture human inferences regarding the evaluativity of different adjectival constructions (POS, EQ, and COMP). We acknowledge that there are limitations, which we hope to address in future studies.

It might not be fine-grained enough to capture the extent to which LMs draw an evaluative inference using the cosine similarity measurement as a proxy. Specifically, our methodology design cannot account for the differences of the similarity scores between the target utterance (a) *Maria is tall* and (b) LM's response *Maria is taller than average*, and those between the target utterance (a) and an *irrelevant* distractor (b′) such as *The Detective is reporting on the height of Maria*, given the prompt *The Detective reported to the Police Chief: "Maria is tall." What can the Chief conclude from this?*. (b′) is entailed by the prompt, although it's not similar to (a) in a vector space. (b) is contextually entailed by the prompt but it's close to (a) in a vector space. This may distract LMs away from the target inference. For future study, we consider using a Natural Language Inference (NLI) model to more directly test the contextual entailment relationship between LMs' response and the target inference.

Typically, LMs are probed by looking at free form continuation or at the probability assigned to different output continuations under the LMs. In this paper, we probed LMs using a question-answering format and measured LMs' performance with similarity scores between LMs' answer and a target inference. But, even with the non-standard methodology, we still found some evidence that LMs do capture human inferences. Our study shows that it's worthwhile to adopt existing sets of human behavioral data in evaluating LMs' weakness and strength. Manipulating the social persona of the "speaker" in a LMs setting is novel yet at preliminary stage. For future work, we hope to expand our current dataset and better our motivation of the sociolinguistic persona design.

5 Appendices

	RELATIVE *tall*		ABSOLUTE *full*	
	POSITIVE *tall*	NEGATIVE *short*	POSITIVE *full*	NEGATIVE *empty*
POS	less evaluative *is tall*		more evaluative *is full*	
EQ	more evaluative *is as tall as*		less evaluative *is as full as*	
COMP	exhibit the same EVAL *is taller than* vs. *is more full than*			

Table 2: Distribution of EVAL implicature - human data: POS is the most evaluative; no difference in polarity (i.e., *positive* and its *negative* antonym) (Brasoveanu and Rett, 2018).

Prompts	GPT-3 response	Macaw response
The Detective reported to the Police Chief: "Maria is tall." What can the Chief conclude from this? [DETECTIVE]	The Police Chief can conclude that Maria is taller than average. The Detective is reporting on the height of Maria.	there's a difference. Maria is tall.
Arthur is clever, smart, quiet, awkward, nerdy, shy and geeky. What does he mean by saying "Maria is tall"? [NERD]	Maria is taller than Arthur. Maria is tall because she is taller than most people.	she's taller than he is. she is tall.
Alex is chill, laid-back, relaxed, easy, cool, friendly, and outgoing. What does he imply by saying "Maria is tall"? [CHILL]	Maria is tall implies that Maria is taller than most people. Maria is taller than Alex.	she is tall. Maria is tall.

Table 3: Example LMs completions with POS as prompt. EQ and COMP were situated in the same prompt frame.

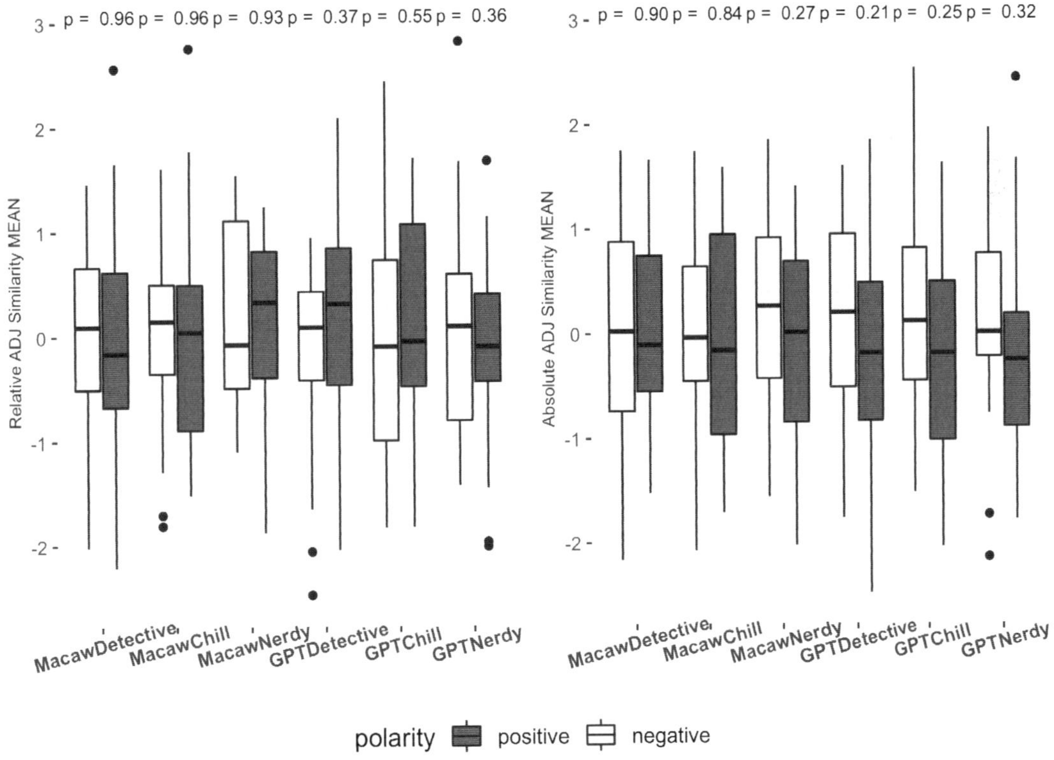

Figure 1: Polarity and LMs' understanding of EVAL. Panels split by adj_class. T-test *p*-values on the top.

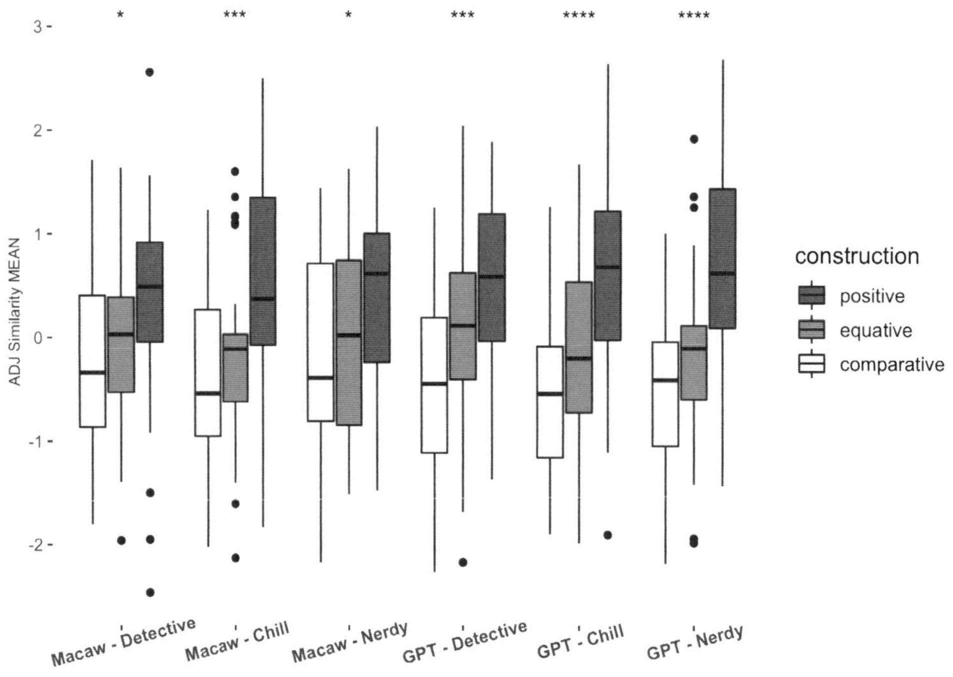

Figure 2: Construction and LMs' understanding of EVAL. Statistical significance (*.05*) on the top.

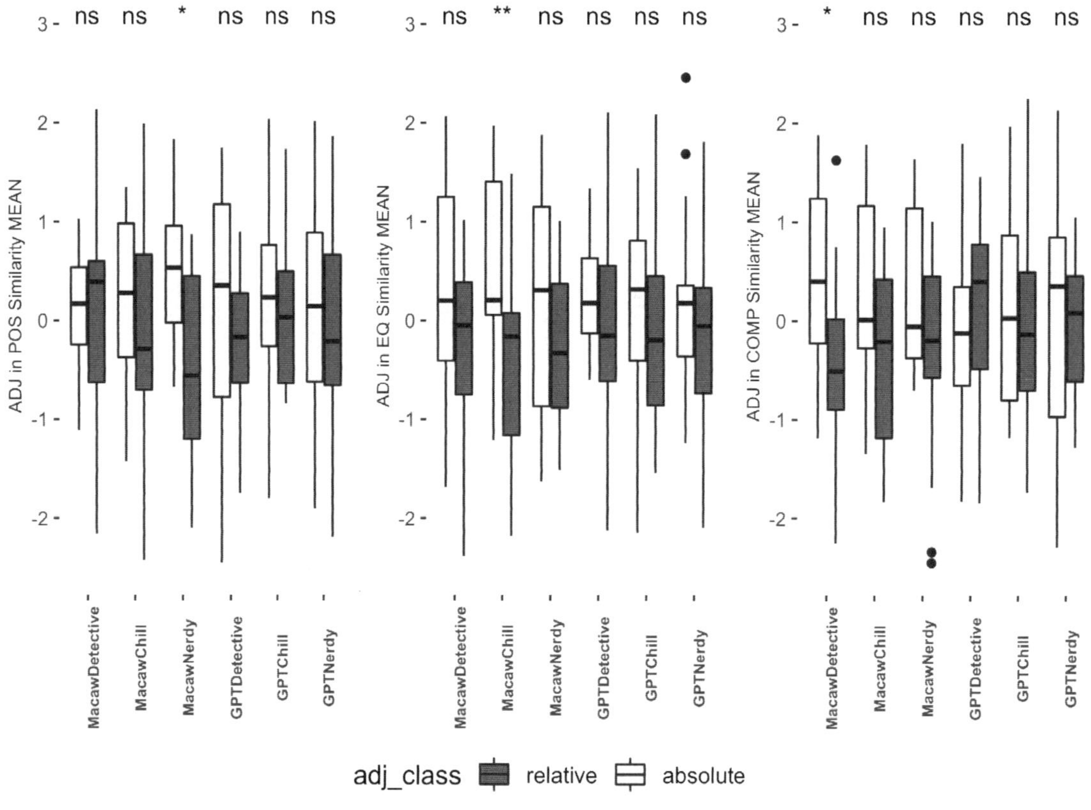

Figure 3: Adj_class and LMs' understanding of EVAL. Panels split by construction. Significance (*.05*) on the top.

References

Andrea Beltrama and Florian Schwarz. 2021. Imprecision, personae, and pragmatic reasoning. In Semantics and Linguistic Theory, volume 31, pages 122–144.

Manfred Bierwisch. 1989. The semantics of gradation. bierwisch, manfred & ewald lang (eds.), dimensional adjectives.

Adrian Brasoveanu and Jessica Rett. 2018. Evaluativity across adjective and construction types: An experimental study. Journal of Linguistics, 54(2):263–329.

Tom Brown, Benjamin Mann, Nick Ryder, Melanie Subbiah, Jared D Kaplan, Prafulla Dhariwal, Arvind Neelakantan, Pranav Shyam, Girish Sastry, Amanda Askell, et al. 2020. Language models are few-shot learners. Advances in neural information processing systems, 33:1877–1901.

Dylan Bumford and Jessica Rett. 2020. Rationalizing evaluativity. In Sinn und Bedeutung 25.

Laura Staum Casasanto. 2008. Does social information influence sentence processing? In Proceedings of the Annual Meeting of the Cognitive Science Society, volume 30.

June Choe, Shayne Sloggett, Masaya Yoshida, and Annette D'onofrio. 2019. Personae in syntactic processing: Socially-specified agents bias expectations of verb transitivity. In Poster presented at the 32nd CUNY Conference on Human Sentence Processing.

M. Cresswell. 1976. The semantics of degree. In B.H. Partee, editor, Montague Grammar, 261-292. Academic Press.

Annette D'onofrio. 2018. Personae and phonetic detail in sociolinguistic signs. Language in Society, 47(4):513–539.

Penelope Eckert. 2008. Variation and the indexical field 1. Journal of sociolinguistics, 12(4):453–476.

Allyson Ettinger. 2020. What BERT is not: Lessons from a new suite of psycholinguistic diagnostics for language models. Transactions of the Association for Computational Linguistics, 8:34–48.

Dan Iter, Jong Yoon, and Dan Jurafsky. 2018. Automatic detection of incoherent speech for diagnosing schizophrenia. In Proceedings of the Fifth Workshop on Computational Linguistics and Clinical Psychology: From Keyboard to Clinic, pages 136–146, New Orleans, LA. Association for Computational Linguistics.

Paloma Jeretic, Alex Warstadt, Suvrat Bhooshan, and Adina Williams. 2020. Are natural language inference models IMPPRESsive? Learning IMPlicature and PRESupposition. In Proceedings of the 58th Annual Meeting of the Association for Computational Linguistics, pages 8690–8705, Online. Association for Computational Linguistics.

William Labov. 2006. The social stratification of English in New York city. Cambridge University Press.

Nancy Niedzielski. 1999. The effect of social information on the perception of sociolinguistic variables. Journal of language and social psychology, 18(1):62–85.

Lalchand Pandia, Yan Cong, and Allyson Ettinger. 2021. Pragmatic competence of pre-trained language models through the lens of discourse connectives. arXiv preprint arXiv:2109.12951.

Robert J Podesva. 2011. Salience and the social meaning of declarative contours: Three case studies of gay professionals. Journal of english linguistics, 39(3):233–264.

Colin Raffel, Noam Shazeer, Adam Roberts, Katherine Lee, Sharan Narang, Michael Matena, Yanqi Zhou, Wei Li, and Peter J. Liu. 2020. Exploring the limits of transfer learning with a unified text-to-text transformer. Journal of Machine Learning Research, 21(140):1–67.

J. Rett. 2008a. Antonymy and evaluativity. In Proceedings of SALT XVII. CLC Publications.

J. Rett. 2008b. Degree Modification in Natural Language. Ph.D. thesis, Rutgers University.

Jessica Rett. 2015. The Semantics of Evaluativity. Oxford University Press.

Jessica Rett. 2019. Manner implicatures and how to spot them. International Review of Pragmatics, in press.

Anna Rogers, Olga Kovaleva, and Anna Rumshisky. 2020. A primer in BERTology: What we know about how BERT works. Transactions of the Association for Computational Linguistics, 8:842–866.

Sebastian Schuster, Yuxing Chen, and Judith Degen. 2020. Harnessing the linguistic signal to predict scalar inferences. In Proceedings of the 58th Annual Meeting of the Association for Computational Linguistics, pages 5387–5403, Online. Association for Computational Linguistics.

Michael Silverstein. 2003. Indexical order and the dialectics of sociolinguistic life. Language & communication, 23(3-4):193–229.

Elizabeth A Strand. 1999. Uncovering the role of gender stereotypes in speech perception. Journal of language and social psychology, 18(1):86–100.

Oyvind Tafjord and Peter Clark. 2021. General-purpose question-answering with Macaw. ArXiv, abs/2109.02593.

Arnim von Stechow. 1984. Comparing semantic theories of comparison. Journal of semantics, 3(3):1–77.

Pragmatic and Logical Inferences in NLI Systems: The Case of Conjunction Buttressing

Paolo Pedinotti
University of Pisa
pedinotti.paolo@gmail.com

Emmanuele Chersoni
The Hong Kong Polytechnic University
emmanuelechersoni@gmail.com

Enrico Santus
Bayer Pharmaceuticals
esantus@gmail.com

Alessandro Lenci
University of Pisa
alessandro.lenci@unipi.it

Abstract

An intelligent system is expected to perform reasonable inferences, accounting for both the literal meaning of a word and the meanings a word can acquire in different contexts. A specific kind of inference concerns the connective *and*, which in some cases gives rise to a temporal succession or causal interpretation in contrast with the logic, commutative one (Levinson, 2000). In this work, we investigate the phenomenon by creating a new dataset for evaluating the interpretation of *and* by NLI systems, which we use to test three Transformer-based models. Our results show that all systems generalize patterns that are consistent with both the logical and the pragmatic interpretation, perform inferences that are inconsistent with each other, and show clear divergences with both theoretical accounts and humans' behavior.

1 Introduction

Implicature is the term used in semantics and pragmatics to describe an inference that goes beyond the literal sense of what is said. Implicatures have received relatively limited attention in computational linguistics, since they are highly dependent on the communication context and on commonsense knowledge. However, the notion of **Generalized Conversational Implicature (GCI)** (Grice, 1975) captures the fact that some of these meaning enrichments are more general than others: They are still dependent on context, but they are also strongly conventionalized and they act as *default inferences*, which are carried out *unless* canceled by additional contextual information.

With this study, we aim at contributing to the research on GCIs in NLP systems by focusing on a specific type of GCI, namely Levinson's **i-implicatures** associated with the conjunction *and* (Levinson, 2000). Studies have noted that *and* is regularly interpreted as a temporal succession or causal connective (from *John repaired the engine and the car started* we understand that the car started as a result of John repairing the engine) (Carston, 1988). This implicature, which is referred to as **conjunction buttressing** by Levinson (2000), contradicts the *commutative* interpretation of *and* traditionally assumed in formal logic and semantics: If *A and B* entails *B after A*, *A and B* is not equivalent to *B and A*. Moreover, the implicature takes place only when the conjuncts express dynamic events, while with static ones *and* preserves the commutative property (e.g., *John was awake and the dog slept* entails *The dog slept and John was awake*).

To address the problem of the scarcity of data for the study of GCIs and conjunction buttressing in particular, we created a dataset for the study of the interpretation of *and* by NLI systems, using manual annotation to obtain quality data and control for features relevant for the implicature according to theoretical accounts. We assigned two different label sets based on a *pragmatic hypothesis* (*and* triggers the implicature) and a *logic* one (*and* is commutative), to distinguish logical vs. pragmatic behavior of the systems.

We tested three Transformer-based NLI systems fine-tuned on MNLI (Williams et al., 2018) on our dataset. We identified systematic inference patterns involving the interpretation of *and* that are common to all three systems. Some of these patterns are in accordance with the pragmatic hypothesis and others with the logic one. We found that the systems make inferences that are inconsistent with each other, and in many cases their interpretation of *and* is different from both the human interpretation and theoretical accounts. To see whether the results are due to biases in the systems' training set, we ran an analysis of MNLI aimed at identifying inference patterns involving *and* that are used by annotators, finding that the inferences generalized by systems are exemplified to varying degrees.

After describing related work in Section 2, in Section 3 we describe how we collected data to

Proceedings of the Second Workshop on Understanding Implicit and Underspecified Language, pages 8 - 16
July 15, 2022 ©2022 Association for Computational Linguistics

assess logical and pragmatic interpretations in NLI systems.[1] Results of the experiments with NLI systems are illustrated in Section 4, along with the analysis on MNLI and the results of a human behavioral study. Conclusions are devoted to suggestions for future work and to the discussion of the limitations of the present work. By highlighting limitations of current systems on our dataset, we argue for a stronger convergence of neural systems for inference and cognitive models of GCIs.

2 Related work

Previous NLP studies on implicatures mostly focused on *scalar implicatures*, inferences involving sets of words that together form a lexical scale (e.g., <*all, some*>). The use of an alternate excludes the other from the interpretation (e.g., *Some of the boys came* +> (implicates) *Not all of the boys came*).

Jeretic et al. (2020) created a large scale dataset of automatically generated sentences following the NLI format, where a premise-hypothesis pair is labeled according to a *logical annotation* (following the logical, literal meaning) and a *pragmatic annotation* (following scalar implicature). The authors measured the accuracy of a BERT model (Devlin et al., 2019) fine-tuned on MNLI according to the logical and the pragmatic annotation. The authors showed that BERT reasoning is more pragmatic than logical for the sentences involving *all* and *some*, even if the results vary depending on how the premise and the hypothesis are built.

Scalar implicatures are not the only type of generalized implicatures. Levinson (2000) proposed a categorization of GCIs based on underlying inferential heuristics related to Grice's maxims of conversation (Grice, 1975). He considered scalar implicatures as an instance of Q-implicatures, a category of GCIs motivated by the principle *Select the informationally strongest paradigmatic alternate that is consistent with the facts*. They are distinguished from **I-implicatures**, motivated by the principle *Assume the richest temporal, causal and referential connections between described situations or events, consistent with what is taken for granted*. A phenomenon in the latter group involves the enrichment of the meaning of *and* (the so-called **conjunction buttressing**): *John repaired the engine* ***and*** *the car starts* implicates ***After*** *John repaired the engine, the car started* (from logical conjunction to temporal succession) and *The car started* ***because*** *John repaired the engine* (from logical conjunction to cause). The inferred meaning of *and* contrasts with the commutative meaning attributed to it in logic and formal semantics.

To our knowledge, Pandia et al. (2021) is the only NLP study dealing with conjuction buttressing: the authors tested if Transformer-based masked language models can predict the temporal connective corresponding to the correct interpretation of the enriched *and*, using the stimuli by Politzer-Ahles et al. (2017). Unlike their study, we created and used labeled data for the evaluation of NLI systems, testing a pragmatic hypothesis (enriched interpretation of *and*) vs. a logical one (commutative interpretation).

3 Data

Given the scarcity of existing resources for GCIs, we collected and annotated new data in NLI format, focusing on different interpretations of the connective *and*. We assigned two different sets of labels, one in accordance with the pragmatic hypothesis (i.e., the implicature is labeled as an entailment) and the other with the logic hypothesis (i.e., only logical inferences are treated as entailments).

Methodology. To obtain data to test the **temporal succession** and the **causal** interpretation of *and*, we first used a multigenre English corpus (UkWac, Ferraresi et al. (2008)) to extract sentences where a main and a subordinate clause are explicitly encoded in a temporal succession or causal relation by a connective (e.g., *Frazier quit* ***before*** *I did*).[2] Then, we replaced the original connective with *and* (*Frazier quit* ***and*** *I did*). The generated and the original sentences are, respectively, the premises and the hypotheses of our experiment (see the first two rows of Table 1). Because the implicature only takes place when two clauses describe events that are presented as a *dynamic process* (Levinson, 2000) (i.e., an event is described as a dynamic situation when it is a process with subparts, such as in *Frazier quit and I did* which implicates succession while *I have two sons and Mary has three* does not), we further manually refined the set to include only those instances. According to the pragmatic hypothesis, the systems should assign the entailment label to these pairs. According to the logical hypothesis, the label is neutral since a literal interpretation of *and* does not entail a temporal

[1]The dataset can be found in the supplementary materials and we will make it available for free use.

[2]See Appendix A for more details about data collection.

Interpretation of *and*	Premise	Hypothesis	Logical label	Pragmatic label
Temporal succession	A and B	B after A	N	E
Causal	A and B	B because A	N	E
Temporal precedence	A and B	B before A	N	C
Temporal synchronous	A and B	B while A	N	C
Commutative (dynamic)	A (dynamic) and B (dynamic)	B (dynamic) and A (dynamic)	E	C
Commutative (static)	A (static) and B (static)	B (static) and A (static)	E	C

Table 1: Dataset structure.

succession or causal relation between events.

From the premises used to test causal interpretation (e.g., *He refused to sign and he lost his job*) we produced new hypotheses where the clauses are linked by other temporal relations contradicting succession, namely **precedence** (***Before*** *he refused to sign, he lost his job*) and **synchronous** (***While*** *he refused to sign, he lost his job*). This is to ensure that systems do not perform an enriched interpretation of *and* that goes in the wrong direction (either temporal or causal). Since the pragmatic interpretation of *and* is temporal succession and this excludes a precedence or synchronous one, we assigned the gold pragmatic label contradiction to these pairs.

We also wanted to test whether NLI systems assign a logical interpretation to the connective *and*, namely **commutativity**. Here we studied the influence of the semantics of the conjuncts: While commutativity is a more natural inference with conjuncts describing static situations (*The rooms are comfortable and the food is super* entails *The food is super and the rooms are comfortable*), with conjuncts describing dynamic situations it is less natural, since it is overridden by the inference stemming from pragmatic enrichment (*He fell off a ladder and he had concussion* contradicts *He had concussion and he fell off a ladder*). To obtain instances of inferences involving the commutativity of *and* with **dynamic conjuncts**, we used the sentences with a causal relation from our dataset. For instance, from the sentence *He had concussion because he fell off a ladder* we generated the premise *He fell off a ladder and he had concussion* and the hypothesis *He had concussion and he fell off a ladder*. For **static conjuncts**, we manually annotated clause pairs linked by *and* in UkWac, and selected only pairs where the main verb of both clauses is stative (*The food is super and the rooms are comfortable*) or has an habitual reading (*Platypus builds nest, and echidna develops pouch*). While commutativity is entailed from the logic perspective, a contradiction would be produced if a pragmatic interpretation of *and* was selected, since temporal succession is not a commutative relation.

	Logical label	Pragmatic label
Temporal succession	0.02	0.94
Causal	0.02	0.98
Temporal precedence	0.07	0.51
Temporal synchronous	0	0
Commutative (dynamic)	1	0
Commutative (static)	1	0

Table 2: Accuracy of the DeBERTa-based system (He et al., 2021) according to the logic and pragmatic label.

Statistics. We collected 653 premise-hypotheses pairs for testing temporal succession interpretation, 270 for testing commutativity (static conjuncts) and 623 for each of causal, precedence, synchronous and commutativity (dynamic), ending up with a total of 3,470 instances.

4 Experiments

Systems. We used our data to evaluate a BERT (Devlin et al., 2019), a RoBERTa (Liu et al., 2019) and a DeBERTa (He et al., 2021) language model fine-tuned on MNLI. For BERT and RoBERTa, we adopted the fine-tuned versions by Poth et al. (2021).[3] We did not perform additional training, as our goal is to test existing systems and our dataset has been built only for evaluation purposes.

Results. We report in Table 2 the results for DeBERTa only, as they are the best ones and there are just slight variations across systems.[4] With *logical* and *pragmatic accuracy*, we refer to accuracy on labels following from the logical and the pragmatic hypotheses respectively.

Results show: a) Pragmatic accuracy close to 1 for Temporal succession and Causal (systems generalize the pattern *A and B* entails *B after A* and *B because A*), but logical accuracy 1 for commutative (systems generalize *A and B* entails *B and A* inde-

[3]See Appendix C for more details about the systems.

[4]Results for all systems can be found in Appendix D

pendent of the semantics of conjuncts); b) Accuracies 0 for temporal synchronous (systems generalize *A and B* entails *B while A*), c) divergent behavior of systems on examples involving a temporal precedence interpretation of *and* (RoBERTa-based: *and* nearly always entails a temporal precedence interpretation; BERT-based: *and* entails a temporal precedence interpretation in 74% of the cases and contradicts it in only 7%; DeBERTa-based: *and* entails temporal precedence in 42% of the cases, and contradicts it in 51%).

Results analysis. We first observe that the inferences drawn by the systems show inconsistent patterns. In many cases the systems assign a succession, precedence and synchronous interpretation to the same pair of conjuncts, which is an overt contradiction. Second, the systems' behavior is not aligned with theoretical accounts of implicatures. Linguistic theory predicts that only a limited set of relations between conjuncts can be inferred (among which succession and cause), while systems consider all the relations we tested as valid inferences. Moreover, while the dynamic event type of the conjuncts is expected to lead to the rejection of the commutative interpretation in favor of an enriched one, systems prefer the commutative pattern irrespective of the context.

MNLI analysis. To see whether results can be explained by biases in the dataset used for training of the systems, we performed an analysis of the MNLI training set aimed at identifying and quantifying inference patterns involving the connective *and* that are used by annotators. To identify examples of pragmatic inference patterns involving the connective *and*, we selected instances where the premise or the hypothesis contains two main clauses linked by *and* using the SpaCy dependency parser (Honnibal and Montani, 2017). We manually inspected 500 out of the 11,208 obtained pairs for cases where the gold label can be explained by assuming the triggering of a pragmatic inference. We found those patterns to be used by MNLI annotators: 26 cases can be explained by assuming an enriched interpretation of *and*. Temporal succession is the most frequent interpretation with 20 cases. Synchronous, causal and inclusion are less present with 3, 1 and 1 cases respectively (see the Appendix B for examples). We found the logic, commutative interpretation of *and* to be much less used for inference by MNLI annotators than the pragmatic one. Out of the 500 examples we analyzed, only 2 can be explained by assuming a commutative interpretation of *and* by annotators (see Appendix B). This analysis shows that inference patterns generalized by systems are exemplified to varying degrees in the training set.

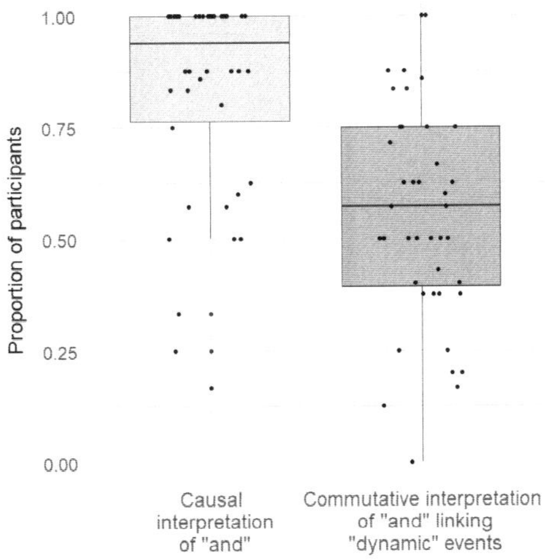

Figure 1: Human behavioral study. The y-axis reports, for each pair, the proportion of participants performing the interpretation on the x-axis.

Human behavioral study. The dataset annotation is based on linguistic theory and expert annotation. To compare it with actual intuitions people have about the meaning of the sentences, we performed a behavioral study using a small subset of premise-hypothesis pairs from the dataset.

Details of the study are given in E. For each of 40 pairs of type Causal, we asked 8 participants to judge if a speaker is implying "B because A" by saying "A and B" or not (that is, we tested if they assign a causal interpretation to *and*). For each of 43 pairs of type Commutativity (dynamic) we asked to judge whether, given a situation where a speaker uses the sentence of form "A and B" and another speaker uses the form "B and A" to describe the same fact, it is possible that both sentences are true at the same time (that is, we tested if a logical, commutative interpretation is assigned to *and*).

The left box in Figure 1 involves pairs of type Causal and shows, for each pair, the proportion of participants assigning a causal interpretation to *and*.[5] If judgments were in perfect agreement with our pragmatic labels, proportion should be 1 for all pairs (0 for logical). In the majority of cases (31 out

[5]The sentences used for the experimental study along with the proportion of participants choosing each answer are provided as a separate file in the supplementary material.

of 40) the proportion is equal to or higher than 0.8. This shows that, in most cases, the responses of almost all participants are in line with our previous annotations. In other cases, there is less support for the causal interpretation, and in a few cases the majority of participants reject it (e.g., *I went to a mass meeting one night and that happened* +> *That happened because I went to a mass meeting one night*, proportion of "Yes": 0.166). We attribute this result to a) Our expert annotation being open to challenge, and b) Limitations of Levinson's theory (possibly there are other factors affecting the pragmatic inference in addition to the situation type of the conjuncts, for example more stereotypical event sequences).

The right box involves pairs of type Commutativity (dynamic) and shows, for each pair, the proportion of participants considering the forms "A and B" and "B and A" true at the same time. If judgments were in perfect agreement with our pragmatic labels, proportion should be 0 for all pairs (1 for logical). Generally, questions receive more variable answers than in the previous group, which can be due to the survey questions being less clear than in the previous case (see E for the form of questions). In some cases, the majority of participants converge on the "Yes" (e.g., *People found them practical and they came into use* and *They came into use and people found them practical* are both true of the same situation according to 85.7% of participants) or the "No" (e.g., *I won an award at 16 for my poetry and I went to Russia* and *I went to Russia and I won an award at 16 for my poetry* are both true of the same situation according to 0% of participants) answer. We argue that answers are determined by the triggering of pragmatic inference (if the inference takes place, the two sentences are not considered true at the same time). The inference takes place differently across our set of pairs, possibly for the reasons we outlined in the paragraph above.

With this experiment, we have explored the distance between our dataset annotation and actual human intuitions about the interpretation of *and*, along with identifying interpretation tendencies.

Confidence scores. To get a more accurate evaluation of the systems and compare their output with human behavioral data, we analyzed the confidence scores of the label entailment for the pairs used for the behavioral study. We found that all systems' scores are concentrated in a small interval near 1 (BERT: [.945, .994], RoBERTa: [.936, .996], DeBERTa: [.950, .999], except for an outlier with score 0.558). The tendency to consistently assign high scores to the entailment label is confirmed by the mean $\overline{x}_n$ and the variance s_n^2 of the samples containing confidence scores of entailment in the whole dataset (BERT: $\overline{x}_n$=.775, s_n^2=.106; RoBERTa: $\overline{x}_n$=.851, s_n^2=.086; DeBERTa: $\overline{x}_n$=.814, s_n^2=.105).

The visualization of the relation between the systems' confidence score of entailment for a given pair and the frequency with which participants consider that pair an example of entailment (given in F) shows no positive correlation. We take the results of this analysis as evidence of a divergence between systems (who consistently choose the entailment label) and humans (who choose entailment label with different frequency across the dataset, showing a variability that does not correlate with the limited variability in the systems' output).

5 Conclusion

We found that NLI systems generalize "pragmatic" and "logical" inference patterns involving the connective *and*. This gives rise to unsatisfactory predictions, since in many cases inferences are not consistent with each other and are not aligned with human ones and theoretical accounts of implicatures. It should be noted that alternative accounts of implicatures exist: For scalar implicatures it has been shown that inference takes place with different strength depending on the context (Degen, 2015). A better assessment of the systems' abilities could be obtained by using implicature strength data. Finally, at this stage we cannot draw general conclusions about whether our results also extend to systems trained on other NLI datasets.

Based on the highlighted limitations of the tested systems, we argue for the need of a stronger convergence of neural systems with theories of GCIs to improve systems' interpretation of *and*. Levinson (2000) proposed that I-implicatures can be explained by assuming that the hearer knows that the speaker tried to achieve her communicative goals by maximizing economy, and thus enriches the interpretation in *stereotypical* ways (since it assumes that the speaker has left stereotypical information unsaid). Stereotypical relations between events in the form of event chains could be automatically collected from texts (Chambers and Jurafsky, 2008) and provided as additional information to systems.

References

Robyn Carston. 1988. Implicature, Explicature, and Truth-Theoretic Semantics. *Mental Representations: The Interface between Language and Reality*, pages 155–181.

Nathanael Chambers and Dan Jurafsky. 2008. Unsupervised Learning of Narrative Event Chains. In *Proceedings of ACL-HLT*.

Judith Degen. 2015. Investigating the Distribution of Some (But Not All) Implicatures Using Corpora and Web-based Methods. *Semantics & Pragmatics*, 8(11):1–55.

Jacob Devlin, Ming-Wei Chang, Kenton Lee, and Kristina Toutanova. 2019. BERT: Pre-training of Deep Bidirectional Transformers for Language Understanding. In *Proceedings of NAACL-HLT*.

Adriano Ferraresi, Eros Zanchetta, Marco Baroni, and Silvia Bernardini. 2008. Introducing and Evaluating UkWaC, a Very Large Web-derived Corpus of English. In *Proceedings of the 4th Web as Corpus Workshop (WAC-4)*, page 47–54.

Herbert Paul Grice. 1975. Logic and Conversation. In *Speech Acts*, pages 41–58. Brill.

Pengcheng He, Xiaodong Liu, Jianfeng Gao, and Weizhu Chen. 2021. DeBERTa: Decoding-enhanced BERT with Disentangled Attention. In *International Conference on Learning Representations*.

Matthew Honnibal and Ines Montani. 2017. spaCy 2: Natural Language Understanding with Bloom Embeddings, Convolutional Neural Networks and Incremental Parsing. *To appear*, 7(1):411–420.

Paloma Jeretic, Alex Warstadt, Suvrat Bhooshan, and Adina Williams. 2020. Are Natural Language Inference Models IMPPRESsive? Learning IMPlicature and PRESupposition. In *Proceedings of ACL*.

Stephen C. Levinson. 2000. *Presumptive Meanings: The Theory of Generalized Conversational Implicature*. The MIT Press, Cambridge, MA.

Yinhan Liu, Myle Ott, Naman Goyal, Jingfei Du, Mandar Joshi, Danqi Chen, Omer Levy, Mike Lewis, Luke Zettlemoyer, and Veselin Stoyanov. 2019. Roberta: A Robustly Optimized BERT Pretraining Approach. *arXiv preprint arXiv:1907.11692*.

Lalchand Pandia, Yan Cong, and Allyson Ettinger. 2021. Pragmatic Competence of Pre-trained Language Models through the Lens of Discourse Connectives. In *Proceedings of CONLL*.

Stephen Politzer-Ahles, Ming Xiang, and Diogo Almeida. 2017. " Before" and" After": Investigating the Relationship between Temporal Connectives and Chronological Ordering Using Event-related Potentials. *PloS One*, 12(4).

Clifton Poth, Jonas Pfeiffer, Andreas Rücklé, and Iryna Gurevych. 2021. What to Pre-Train on? Efficient Intermediate Task Selection. In *Proceedings of EMNLP*.

Rashmi Prasad, Nikhil Dinesh, Alan Lee, Eleni Miltsakaki, Livio Robaldo, Aravind Joshi, and Bonnie Webber. 2008. The Penn Discourse TreeBank 2.0. In *Proceedings of LREC*.

Adina Williams, Nikita Nangia, and Samuel Bowman. 2018. A Broad-Coverage Challenge Corpus for Sentence Understanding through Inference. In *Proceedings of NAACL-HLT*.

A Details about Data Collection

Using the SpaCy dependency parser (`https://spacy.io/`), we extracted sentences from UkWac (Ferraresi et al., 2008) matching the dependency pattern CONNECTIVE-*mark*-V-*advcl*-V-*ROOT*, where CONNECTIVE is a connective that unambiguously signal the discourse relation of interest (*before*, *after* and *once* for temporal succession, *because* for causal) and V is a verb according to the SpaCy POS tagger. We selected clauses linked by connectives that are unambiguous in term of their discourse function according to the English Penn Discourse Treebank (Prasad et al., 2008).

For our experiments, we used the SpaCy pipeline `en_core_web_s` from the most recent version 3.2. SpaCy is licensed under the MIT license.

UkWac is a large-scale corpus (>2 billion words) created with texts from URLs in the `.uk` web domain. URLs were selected based on the presence of a pair of words, where pairs are from a list created by choosing random medium-frequency words from BNC (written and spoken version) and a vocabulary list for foreign learner of English. This strategy ensures variety of content. As a result, the corpus covers various domains and demographic groups. The prevailing language is British English, but the presence of other variety of English cannot be excluded. The corpus is freely downloadable at `https://wacky.sslmit.unibo.it/`.

B Analysis of MNLI

Examples of pragmatic interpretation of *and*. Temporal succession interpretation: *Thorn turned and left* entails *Thorn left after he turned* (pairID: 17201c). Temporal synchronous interpretation: *The man roared out and cleaved off the demon's other arm* entails *The man made a loud noise as he injured the demon* (pairID: 35017e). Causal interpretation: *After 37 years of rule, Solomon died* *and the kingdom was split between the northern and southern tribes* entails *Solomon was the ruler for 37 years and his death resulted in the divide of the kingdom between north and south* (pairID: 56084e). Temporal inclusion interpretation: *we came here and they had parking lots in the schools and i couldn't understand it you know all the kids had cars* entails *I was surprised to see that all the kids had cars when we came here* (pairID: 2744e).

Examples of commutative interpretation of *and*. *Several years ago a radio broke in my car and i never i got out of the habit of listening to the radio* entails *Several years ago a radio broke in my car and i never i got out of the habit of listening to the radio and I always stuck to the habit of listening to the radio, and mine broke* (pairID: 24186e).

C Systems details

The three systems we used for our experiments are Transformer models fine-tuned on MultiNLI (Williams et al., 2018). MNLI was built based on the following procedure. First, text sources of ten different genres (including written and spoken speech) are used to select sentences that are used as premises. Sources are from the Open American National Corpus and a selection of works of contemporary fiction. Then, a crowdworker is asked to produce a hypothesis for each NLI label (entailment, neutral, contradiction). Finally, other crowdworkers are asked to assign a label to each premise-hypothesis pair and a gold label is assigned based on the majority of labels. The corpus comes with a training/test/development split (392,702/ 20,000/ 20,000 examples respectively). MNLI can be freely used and may be modified and redistributed. The corpus is released under several licenses (cf. Williams et al. (2018) for details).

The three systems can be downloaded freely from `https://huggingface.co/` and are `bert-base-uncased-pf-mnli` (Poth et al., 2021), `roberta-base-pf-mnli` (Poth et al., 2021) and `deberta-v2-xlarge-mnli` (He et al., 2021). `deberta-v2-xlarge-mnli` is licensed under the MIT license. Details about the tested systems are provided in Table 3. We refer the reader to the original paper for further details.

D Results for all Systems

E Survey details

Platform. We launched the survey on Prolific Academic (`https://www.prolific.co/`).

	bert-base-uncased-pf-mnli	roberta-base-pf-mnli	deberta-v2-xlarge-mnli
Paper	Poth et al. 2021	Poth et al. 2021	He et al. 2021
Number of parameters (Language Model)	110M	125M	900M
Computational budget		8 × 32GB V100 GPUs	6 × 96GB V100 GPUs
Fine-tuning strategy	Adapter-based	Adapter-based	Scale-invariant
MNLI accuracy	84.2	87.5	91.7

Table 3: Details about the tested systems.

	Logical label	Pragmatic label
Temporal succession	0.02	0.81
Causal	0.03	0.97
Temporal precedence	0.19	0.07
Temporal synchronous	0	0.02
Commutative (dynamic)	1	0
Commutative (static)	1	0

Table 4: Results for the BERT-based system (Poth et al., 2021).

Participation requirements. Participants were required to a) Be born in the U.S., b) Be a U.S. citizen, c) Be in the U.S. at the time of the test, d) Have English as their first language, e) Have an approval rate of previous studies on Prolific between 90% and 100%, f) Have completed at least 50 tests on Prolific. We used Prolific's internal screening system for excluding participants who did not meet the requirements.

Survey structure. Each test consisted of 20 questions. Possible answers for each question in a survey were "Yes" and "No". 5 questions targeted the pragmatic interpretation of the *and* connective, 5 questions targeted the logical (commutative) interpretation, and the other 10 were comprehension question. Each question targeting the **pragmatic** interpretation of *and* has the following structure:

- Imagine that a speaker says PREMISE. In your opinion, is the speaker implying HY-

	Logical label	Pragmatic label
Temporal succession	0.01	0.91
Causal	0.01	0.98
Temporal precedence	0	0.07
Temporal synchronous	0	0
Commutative (dynamic)	0.98	0.02
Commutative (static)	0.98	0.02

Table 5: Results for the RoBERTa-based system (Poth et al., 2021).

POTHESIS?

PREMISE and HYPOTHESIS are examples of type "Causal" from the dataset presented in this article (an example of question is: *Imagine that a speaker says "I got bored in the first year and I dropped out of university". In your opinion, is the speaker implying "I dropped out of university because I got bored in the first year"?*).

Each question targeting the **logical (commutative)** interpretation of *and* has the following structure:

- Imagine that two speakers A and B know the same fact and are telling it. A says PREMISE, and we know she is telling things as they actually happened. Now imagine B says HYPOTHESIS. Is B also telling things as they happened?

PREMISE and HYPOTHESIS are examples of type "Commutativity (dynamic situation)" from the dataset presented in this article (an example of question is: *7. Imagine that two speakers A and B know the same fact and are telling it. A says "IBM used Intel and Intel became standard ", and we know she is telling things as they actually happened. Now imagine B says "Intel became standard and IBM used Intel". Is B also telling things as they happened?*).

Comprehension questions were added to a) Prevent participant from associating questions of a given form with a given answer, b) Mitigate the bias of questions of a given form towards a given answer type (given our previous annotation, we expected questions targeting pragmatic interpretation to have "Yes" as prevailing answer), c) Prompt participants to pay more attention to the meaning of the sentences in the survey, and d) Exclude from the final dataset the answer of participant who are suspected of not comprehending the task or not paying the right attention to the questions.

The comprehension questions have the same form of the other questions, but instead of targeting inference patterns involving the interpretation of *and*, they asked participants to make simple inferences based on other elements of sentences. Examples were inferences based on presuppositions (e.g., *Imagine that a speaker says "Europe tried to sweep itself clean of Jews and it came into existence". In your opinion, is the speaker implying that there were Jews in Europe?*), paraphrases (*Imagine that two speakers A and B know the same fact and are telling it. A says "Phillip adamantly and persistently refused to pay her a penny piece and she succeeded", and we know she is telling things as they actually happened. Now imagine B says "She was not given a penny by Philip and she succeeded". Is B also telling things as they happened?*), contradictions based on negation or antonyms (*Imagine that a speaker says "Christian voice intimidated 1/3 of the venues into dropping out and the tour became financially impossible". In your opinion, is the speaker implying "Christian voice intimidated 1/3 of the venues into dropping out and the tour became financially sustainable"?*).

Since they involve straightforward inference patterns and they are not the focus of the experiment, we had gold standard answers for comprehension questions, which we used to exclude answers of participants from the dataset.

To ensure participants made choices based on their intuitions, no examples were provided in the instructions.

Number of participants and reward. Each survey was presented to 8 participants. 9 surveys were created in total, for a total of 72 participants taking part in the experiment. Participants were not allowed to take part in more than one survey. They received a reward of 0.55£ (0.65€, 0.67$).

Requirements for inclusion in the dataset. In order for a participant answers to be included in the final dataset, the participant must give the gold standard answer to at least 7 of the 10 comprehension question in the survey. This strategy led to the exclusion of the answers of 5 out of 72 participants.

F Systems' confidence scores for sentences from the experimental study

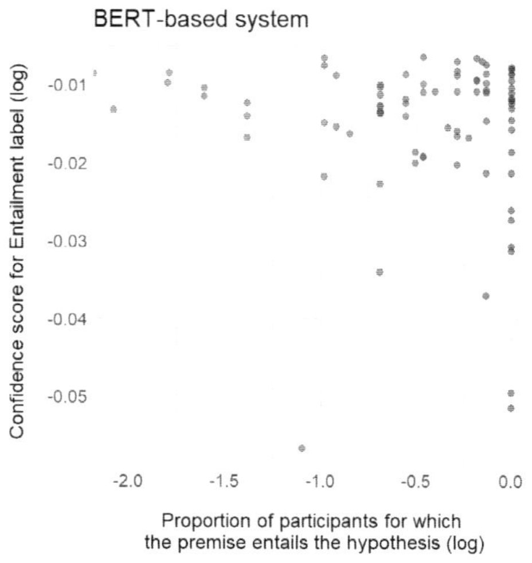
BERT-based system
Confidence score for Entailment label (log)
-0.01
-0.02
-0.03
-0.04
-0.05
-2.0
-1.5
-1.0
-0.5
0.0
Proportion of participants for which the premise entails the hypothesis (log)

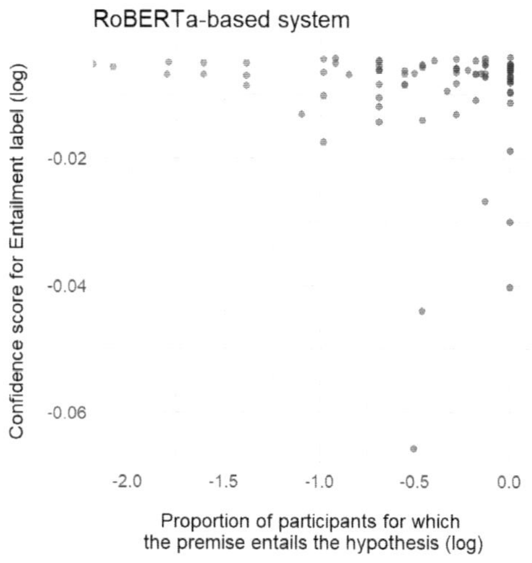
RoBERTa-based system
Confidence score for Entailment label (log)
-0.02
-0.04
-0.06
-2.0
-1.5
-1.0
-0.5
0.0
Proportion of participants for which the premise entails the hypothesis (log)

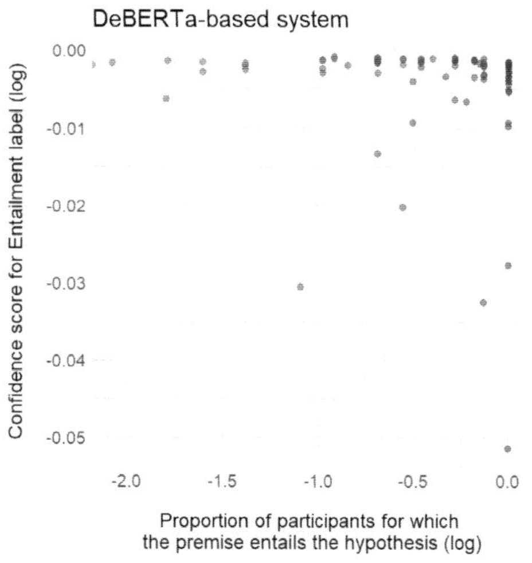
DeBERTa-based system
Confidence score for Entailment label (log)
0.00
-0.01
-0.02
-0.03
-0.04
-0.05
-2.0
-1.5
-1.0
-0.5
0.0
Proportion of participants for which the premise entails the hypothesis (log)

"Devils Are in the Details": Annotating Specificity of Clinical Advice from Medical Literature

Yingya Li
School of Information Studies
Syracuse University
yli48@syr.edu

Bei Yu
School of Information Studies
Syracuse University
byu@syr.edu

Abstract

Prior studies have raised concerns over specificity issues in clinical advice. Lacking specificity — explicitly discussed detailed information — may affect the quality and implementation of clinical advice in medical practice. In this study, we developed and validated a fine-grained annotation schema to describe different aspects of specificity in clinical advice extracted from medical research literature. We also presented our initial annotation effort and discussed future directions towards an NLP-based specificity analysis tool for summarizing and verifying the details in clinical advice.

1 Introduction

In medical literature, authors often explain clinical implications after presenting their research findings. For example, "Results of this post-hoc analysis suggest that LEV may be a suitable option for initial monotherapy for patients aged $\geq$ 60 years with newly diagnosed epilepsy" (Pohlmann-Eden et al., 2016). Clinical advice like this can influence health researchers and practitioners on specific medical practices. Hence, it is an important information service to retrieve and analyze clinical advice from medical literature.

Prior studies have identified some quality issues that may affect the implementation of clinical advice. One concern is the lack of specificity. Two studies have compared the implementation outcomes of professionally-designed clinical guidelines with different levels of specificity, and found that concrete and precise descriptions resulted in higher adoption rate (Michie and Johnston, 2004; Michie and Lester, 2005). Clinical advice in medical literature also varies in specificity levels. For example, advice sentences appeared in abstracts tend to be less specific compared to those in discussions, where more space is available for explaining the details (Li and Yu, 2022).

To better retrieve and summarize clinical advice from medical literature, this study aims to develop a taxonomy of specifics in clinical advice, such that they may be retrieved and compared in finer granularity. We developed and validated an annotation schema that can partition a clinical advice sentence to multiple elements: 1) agents; 2) substantial qualifications or elaborations; 3) chain of reasoning; 4) confidence. This annotation schema was developed based on medical research on clinical guidelines and NLP research on modeling specificity as a language construct.

We also discussed the future directions for computationally modeling specificity of clinical advice in medical literature. Such specificity analysis tool can be used for downstream applications such as detecting quality issues of clinical advice. For example, one study raised severe concern that many recommendations for clinical practice were not supported by findings in the conclusions (Yavchitz et al., 2016). The problem is more severe in abstracts than in discussions. Since abstracts are much more accessible than full-text articles, the "spins" in abstracts are also more harmful than those in discussions (Boutron et al., 2014). An NLP-based specificity analysis tool can help compare recommendation details against available evidence, or compare similar recommendations in fine-granularity.

2 Related Work

Specificity is an important concept in both clinical practice and claim analyses. In medical domain, specificity is defined narrowly, focusing on the detailed information regarding clinical practice and health-related behavior changes. For example, Shekelle et al. (2000) defined a specific guideline as "creates clinical appropriate criteria for a large number of clinically detailed patient presentations; it does not force consensus" (p.1431). Similarly, Michie and Lester (2005) argued that specific

Proceedings of the Second Workshop on Understanding Implicit and Underspecified Language, pages 17 - 21
July 15, 2022 ©2022 Association for Computational Linguistics

clinical guidelines give "detailed advice on which performance is appropriate in which situation and in what patient group and determining which factors, or conditions should be taken into account" (p. 367). Note that clinical guidelines used in practice are usually developed by professional institutions such as National Institute for Clinical Excellence (NICE). They are usually more comprehensive and specific than the clinical advice from individual research papers.

Compared to the narrow definition in clinical domain, specificity is defined more broadly in the NLP field, referring to how much detailed information is included in a statement. Depending on the text domains, researchers have proposed different taxonomies to define specificity. For example, in education domain, the specificity of classroom discussions was defined based on four aspects: "involves one character or scene", "gives substantial qualifications or elaboration", "uses content-specific vocabulary", and "provides a chain of reasoning" (Lugini and Litman, 2017). Similarly, arguments in student essays were assigned specificity scores based on occurrence of qualifiers, references to supporting components, hypotheses, and real-world examples (Carlile et al., 2018). Specificity in other domains was defined quite differently. For example, the specificity of pledges of election manifestos were labelled based on expressions of moral values, intangible goals and outcomes, commitment to the maintenance of functioning policy, means and details to achieve the objectives (Subramanian et al., 2019). The specificity in social media posts was defined based on their references to specific person, object or event (Gao et al., 2019).

Although the exact aspects applied to describe specificity differ by domains, they usually cover the anwers to questions about who, what, when, where, why, and how. Since the clinical domain and the education domain are most relevant to our task, we defined our annotation schema by combining the definitions from these two domains.

3 Data and Annotation Schema

3.1 Dataset

In this study, we used an open-access dataset on health advice, which contains a sample of 10,848 sentences extracted from abstracts and discussion sections in medical research papers, in which 2,748 sentences were annotated as health advice (Li et al., 2021). The research papers include different study designs, including randomized controlled trials and four types of observational studies, including cross-sectional, case-control, retrospective, and prospective studies. We sampled sentences from all study designs to ensure the annotation schema is generalizable. We first sampled 100 advice sentences to develop the annotation schema and finalize the definition of each concept. We then sampled another 100 advice sentences to evaluate the inter-coder agreement on the finalized annotation schema.

3.2 Annotating Clinical and Non-clinical Advice

In the health advice dataset (Li et al., 2021), the annotated health advice may recommend clinical intervention and practice ("clinical advice") or simply raise awareness and call for actions for certain health behavior or policy change ("non-clinical advice"). The latter type tends to use vague verbs such as "address" and "encourage" instead of concrete description of interventions. In this study, we focus on clinical advice. Hence, the first step in the annotation is to distinguish clinical vs. non-clinical advice. Clinical advice will be further annotated with specificity aspects. Occasionally, we encountered a sentence with serious semantic ambiguity, and labelled it as incomprehensive.

Drawing on prior specificity annotations on clinical guidelines, we adopted two key aspects that also appear in clinical advice in medical literature: "agents" and "substantial qualifications or elaborations". In addition, we found two aspects in clinical advice from medical literature but are absent in clinical guidelines: "chain of reasoning" and "confidence". Diffrent from clinical guidelines that focus on what to do only, clinical advice from research papers sometimes includes explanations on the reason of why a recommendation was made. Therefore, we added "chain of reasoning". This concept is borrowed from specificity annotation in the education domain (Lugini and Litman, 2017).

In addition, authors often expressed their confidence in clinical advice using words like "possible", "may","can", and "is", based on the evidence level. This concept is relevant to the "strong/weak advice" concept in the original health advice data set, or prior studies that distinguished "implicit/explicit advice" (Sumner et al., 2014). These prior studies aimed for categorical definition of the advice strength, and they cover both clinical and non-clinical advice. In this study, we use the concept

Advice Type	Description	Example Sentence and Specificity Annotation
Non-clinical Advice	Health advice that aims to raise awareness or calls for actions for health-related behavioral changes. The outcome of the action is not directly measurable. Use verbs such as "address", "encourage", and "ensure".	1. Special attention is required in such patients while doing treatment planning. 2. We conclude that it is important to encourage physical activity in this population.
Clinical Advice	Health advice that provides clear actionable suggestions for medical practice and policy changes. The advice contains precise and concrete description for the treatment or intervention that needs to be taken.	3. Therefore, intraoperative antifibrinolysis may not be indicated in routine cardiac surgery when other blood-saving techniques are adopted. **Annotation**: agent (N/A), intervention ("intraoperative antifibrinolysis"), target (N/A), goal ("routine cardiac surgery when other blood-saving techniques are adopted"), chain of reasoning (N/A), confidence ("may not be indicated in") 4. Therefore, due to the cost, possible side effects, and the limited saving of homologous blood, intraoperative antifibrinolytic therapy may not be indicated in routine cardiac surgery. **Annotation**: agent (N/A), intervention ("intraoperative antifibrinolytic therapy"), target (N/A), goal ("routine cardiac surgery"), chain of reasoning ("therefore, due to the cost, possible side effects, and the limited saving of homologous blood"), confidence ("may not be indicated in")

Table 1: Specificity annotation schema and sentence examples.

	RCTs	Cross-Sectional	Case-Control	Retrospective	Prospective	Total	Percentage
Clinical	27	15	17	22	19	100	50.0%
Non-clinical	13	25	22	18	20	98	49.0%
Total	40	40	39	40	39	200	

Table 2: Distribution of clinical and non-clinical advice in annotated corpus.

"confidence" to emphasize that we aim to identify the phrases that describe confidence level in clinical advice only.

Overall, we defined specificity from the following four dimensions: "agents", "substantial qualifications or elaborations", "chain of reasoning", and "confidence". Table 1 shows the definition and sentence examples of the annotation schema.

Agents: the party to carry out the recommended clinical practice, such as health practitioners or organizations.

Substantial qualifications or elaborations: concrete and precise details in health advice that depicts what, who, when, where, and how information to assist implementation of actionable clinical practice. We further categorized it by the following sub-dimensions:

Intervention: the details of treatment, such as therapy procedures, doses and usage

Target: the party to receive the recommended intervention, usually patients, sometimes including demographical details or body parts to be treated.

Goal: illness/symptom that the intervention aims to treat, or another treatment that it aims to support.

Chain of reasoning: reasons for the clinical advice, normally indicated by linguistic cues such as "although", "as long as" and "since", when health researchers admitting a fact or showing contrasts in recommendations.

Confidence: the level of confidence researchers have when giving the advice.

3.3 Inter-coder Agreement

To test the validity of the proposed schema, a sample of 100 advice sentences were randomly selected for inter-coder agreement evaluation. We applied disproportionate stratified sampling to get 20 advice sentences from each of the 5 study designs. Two annotators with the education backgrounds of linguistics and information science each labelled the 100 sentences for clinical advice and specificity. The overall Cohen's Kappa agreement (Cohen, 1960) on annotating clinical and non-clinical advice was 0.88, indicating a near-perfect inter-coder agreement (McHugh, 2012). The agreement on each of the specificity dimensions were: agent (0.98), intervention (0.93), target (0.91), goal (0.87), chain of reasoning (0.91), and confidence

Specifics	Count	Percentage
Agent	3	3.0%
Intervention	100	100.0%
Target	58	58.0%
Goal	88	88.0%
Reasoning	25	25.0%
Confidence	100	100.0%

Table 3: Distribution of the advice details on each dimension of specificity.

(0.93). Disagreed cases were later resolved by the two annotators through discussion.

3.4 Specifics in Clinical Advice

We annotated 200 health advice sentences in total for schema development and validation. Excluding two incomprehensible sentences, 100 were "clinical advice", and 98 were "non-clinical" advice. Table 2 shows their distributions across different study designs. The almost equal distribution of clinical and non-clinical advice suggests that researchers tend to give both advice for clinical practice/interventions and advice that calls for general health-related behavior changes. However, when zooming into the different study deigns, we noted that RCTs have a higher percentage of clinical advice (67.5%) than the observational studies followed by retrospective (55.0%), prospective (47.5%), case-control (42.5%), and cross-sectional studies (37.5%), indicating that researchers are more likely to give clinical advice in studies with higher evidence levels. The quality of clinical advice given in observational studies was more often questioned by the research community (Cofield et al., 2010).

Among the 100 clinical advice sentences, "intervention", "confidence" and "goal" are most often mentioned. Different from professionally-designed clinical guidelines, "agent" in medical literature is almost always omitted, and "target" is omitted over 40% of times. Reasoning is also not often provided (25%). See Table 3 for the aspect distribution.

With the fine-grained specificity annotation, we can then compare details of recommendations against evidence strength or compare different versions of similar recommendations. For example, in Table 1, examples 3 and 4 appear in the same research paper but different sections. The annotations show that the first sentence provides a more specific goal, while the second sentence provides reasoning.

4 Towards Computational Modeling of Specificity

The explosive growth of research output and restricted human capacities in information processing and decision making calls for an NLP-based specificity analysis tool to synthesize and aggregate the scientific evidence and clinical recommendations in research publications. The developed annotation schema may then be used to develop automatic prediction models for clinical advice specifics classification and specifics extraction. Based on the occurrence for each specificity dimension, we could frame the task as a sentence-level classification task and to computationally model the specificity level in each advice sentences. Utilizing the annotated details under each specificity aspect, the task could also be framed as an information extraction one. Information extraction tools could be developed to extract the details of each recommendation. For example, simple rule-based approaches using regular expressions (Savova et al., 2010a) may identify the aspects of agents and targets. Existing NLP tools for medical concepts (e.g. Savova et al., 2010b; Zhou et al., 2019; Zhang et al., 2021) and clinical relation extractions based on pre-trained language models such as BERT (Roy and Pan, 2021) may further identify other specificity aspects in the develop schema. After extracting the specifics explicitly mentioned in each recommendation, we could compare different versions of semantically similar recommendations across the specifics to detect the inconsistent or exaggerated clinical advice in research literature.

5 Conclusion

In this work we presented a fine-grained annotation schema for describing specificity in clinical advice extracted from medical research literature. An inter-coder agreement check shows the proposed annotation schema reached almost perfect agreement in all dimensions. The annotation schema could be used to develop gold-standard dataset that can be used to develop NLP models for identifying fine-grained specificity aspects in clinical advice, and to support downstream applications such as summarizing clinical advice or fact checking.

Acknowledgement

This research is supported by the US National Science Foundation under grant 1952353 and the Syracuse University CUSE Grant.

References

Isabelle Boutron, Douglas G Altman, Sally Hopewell, Francisco Vera-Badillo, Ian Tannock, and Philippe Ravaud. 2014. Impact of spin in the abstracts of articles reporting results of randomized controlled trials in the field of cancer: the spiin randomized controlled trial. *Journal of Clinical Oncology*, 32(36):4120–4126.

Winston Carlile, Nishant Gurrapadi, Zixuan Ke, and Vincent Ng. 2018. Give me more feedback: Annotating argument persuasiveness and related attributes in student essays. In *Proceedings of the 56th Annual Meeting of the Association for Computational Linguistics (Volume 1: Long Papers)*, pages 621–631.

Stacey S Cofield, Rachel V Corona, and David B Allison. 2010. Use of causal language in observational studies of obesity and nutrition. *Obesity facts*, 3(6):353–356.

Jacob Cohen. 1960. A coefficient of agreement for nominal scales. *Educational and psychological measurement*, 20(1):37–46.

Yifan Gao, Yang Zhong, Daniel Preoţiuc-Pietro, and Junyi Jessy Li. 2019. Predicting and analyzing language specificity in social media posts. In *Proceedings of the AAAI Conference on Artificial Intelligence*, volume 33, pages 6415–6422.

Yingya Li, Jun Wang, and Bei Yu. 2021. Detecting health advice in medical research literature. In *Proceedings of the 2021 Conference on Empirical Methods in Natural Language Processing*, pages 6018–6029.

Yingya Li and Bei Yu. 2022. Advice giving in medical research literature. In *International Conference on Information*, pages 261–272. Springer.

Luca Lugini and Diane Litman. 2017. Predicting specificity in classroom discussion. In *Proceedings of the 12th Workshop on Innovative Use of NLP for Building Educational Applications*, pages 52–61.

Mary L McHugh. 2012. Interrater reliability: the kappa statistic. *Biochemia medica*, 22(3):276–282.

S Michie and Kathryn Lester. 2005. Words matter: increasing the implementation of clinical guidelines. *BMJ Quality & Safety*, 14(5):367–370.

Susan Michie and Marie Johnston. 2004. Changing clinical behaviour by making guidelines specific. *Bmj*, 328(7435):343–345.

Bernd Pohlmann-Eden, Anthony G Marson, Matthias Noack-Rink, Francisco Ramirez, Azita Tofighy, Konrad J Werhahn, Imane Wild, and Eugen Trinka. 2016. Comparative effectiveness of levetiracetam, valproate and carbamazepine among elderly patients with newly diagnosed epilepsy: subgroup analysis of the randomized, unblinded komet study. *BMC neurology*, 16(1):1–12.

Arpita Roy and Shimei Pan. 2021. Incorporating medical knowledge in bert for clinical relation extraction. In *Proceedings of the 2021 Conference on Empirical Methods in Natural Language Processing*, pages 5357–5366.

Guergana K Savova, Jin Fan, Zi Ye, Sean P Murphy, Jiaping Zheng, Christopher G Chute, and Iftikhar J Kullo. 2010a. Discovering peripheral arterial disease cases from radiology notes using natural language processing. In *AMIA Annual Symposium Proceedings*, volume 2010, page 722. American Medical Informatics Association.

Guergana K Savova, James J Masanz, Philip V Ogren, Jiaping Zheng, Sunghwan Sohn, Karin C Kipper-Schuler, and Christopher G Chute. 2010b. Mayo clinical text analysis and knowledge extraction system (ctakes): architecture, component evaluation and applications. *Journal of the American Medical Informatics Association*, 17(5):507–513.

Paul G Shekelle, Richard L Kravitz, Jennifer Beart, Michael Marger, Mingming Wang, and Martin Lee. 2000. Are nonspecific practice guidelines potentially harmful? a randomized comparison of the effect of nonspecific versus specific guidelines on physician decision making. *Health services research*, 34(7):1429.

Shivashankar Subramanian, Trevor Cohn, and Timothy Baldwin. 2019. Deep ordinal regression for pledge specificity prediction. In *Proceedings of the 2019 Conference on Empirical Methods in Natural Language Processing and the 9th International Joint Conference on Natural Language Processing (EMNLP-IJCNLP)*, pages 1729–1740.

Petroc Sumner, Solveiga Vivian-Griffiths, Jacky Boivin, Andy Williams, Christos A Venetis, Aimée Davies, Jack Ogden, Leanne Whelan, Bethan Hughes, Bethan Dalton, et al. 2014. The association between exaggeration in health related science news and academic press releases: retrospective observational study. *Bmj*, 349.

Amélie Yavchitz, Philippe Ravaud, Douglas G Altman, David Moher, Asbjørn Hrobjartsson, Toby Lasserson, and Isabelle Boutron. 2016. A new classification of spin in systematic reviews and meta-analyses was developed and ranked according to the severity. *Journal of clinical epidemiology*, 75:56–65.

Yuhao Zhang, Yuhui Zhang, Peng Qi, Christopher D Manning, and Curtis P Langlotz. 2021. Biomedical and clinical english model packages for the stanza python nlp library. *Journal of the American Medical Informatics Association*, 28(9):1892–1899.

Xin Zhou, Yanshan Wang, Sunghwan Sohn, Terry M Therneau, Hongfang Liu, and David S Knopman. 2019. Automatic extraction and assessment of lifestyle exposures for alzheimer's disease using natural language processing. *International journal of medical informatics*, 130:103943.

Searching for PETs: Using Distributional and Sentiment-Based Methods to Find Potentially Euphemistic Terms

Patrick Lee and **Martha Gavidia** and **Anna Feldman** and **Jing Peng**
Montclair State University
Montclair, New Jersey
{leep6, gavidiam1 feldmana, pengj}@montclair.edu

Abstract

This paper presents a linguistically driven proof of concept for finding *potentially euphemistic terms*, or PETs. Acknowledging that PETs tend to be commonly used expressions for a certain range of sensitive topics, we make use of distributional similarities to select and filter phrase candidates from a sentence and rank them using a set of simple sentiment-based metrics. We present the results of our approach tested on a corpus of sentences containing euphemisms, demonstrating its efficacy for detecting single and multi-word PETs from a broad range of topics. We also discuss future potential for sentiment-based methods on this task.

1 Introduction

Euphemisms are mild or indirect expressions used in place of harsher or more offensive ones. They can be used to show politeness when discussing sensitive or taboo topics (Bakhriddionova, 2021) such as saying *passed away* instead of *died*, or as a way to make unpleasant or unappealing things sound better (Karam, 2011), such as *ethnic cleansing* instead of *genocide*. They can even be used as a means to conceal the truth (Rababah, 2014); for example, saying *enhanced interrogation techniques* but meaning *torture*. Euphemisms pose a challenge to natural language processing due to this figurative behavior, but also because they can have a literal interpretation in certain contexts. Furthermore, humans may not agree on what a euphemism is (Gavidia et al., 2022). Thus, we consider any words/phrases used in this nature to be a *Potentially Euphemistic Term* (PET).

In this paper, we present a proof of concept for finding PETs in an input sentence, and apply it to a novel euphemism corpus (Gavidia et al., 2022)[1]. We base our approach on several linguistic intuitions: (1) PETs tend to be commonly used expressions about a certain range of sensitive topics, (2) humans make a conscious lexical choice to convey politeness and formality and (3) because of their linguistic function, PETs should result in greater sentiment shifts when replaced by their literal interpretations; we experiment with distributionally similar alternatives as a source of such interpretations. Leveraging a variety of existing tools (Gensim's Phrases (Rehurek and Sojka, 2011), word2vec classes (Mikolov et al., 2013), and roBERTa (Liu et al., 2019)), we implement a simple algorithm to extract, filter, and rank PET candidates. Despite its simplicity, our approach is able to identify the target euphemism as one of the top two phrase candidates for 725 out of 1382 sentences in our test dataset. It also shows promising results in identifying PETs that were not originally marked, as well as for sentences outside our dataset. We believe our results and subsequent discussion are an important baseline for using distributional and sentiment-based methods for detecting euphemisms.

The structure of the paper is as follows: in Section 2, we discuss related work surrounding euphemisms. Section 3 provides details on the text data used, Section 4 describes our approach broken down into 4 stages: *phrase extraction, phrase filtering, phrase paraphrasing and phrase ranking*. Section 5 includes our results and a quantitative and qualitative analysis, and Section 6 concludes with future work.

2 Related Work

Computational approaches to processing euphemisms (Felt and Riloff, 2020; Zhu et al., 2021; Zhu and Bhat, 2021; Magu and Luo, 2018; Kapron-King and Xu, 2021; Gavidia et al., 2022) have shown much promise, but the dynamic nature of euphemisms remains an obstacle. A euphemism annotation task conducted by Gavidia et al. (2022) shows that the inherent ambiguity of euphemisms

[1]Our code is available at `https://github.com/marsgav/PETDetection`.

Proceedings of the Second Workshop on Understanding Implicit and Underspecified Language, pages 22 - 32
July 15, 2022

leads to low agreement in what qualifies as a euphemism. Through this task, the researchers found that some euphemisms are used so often to discuss sensitive topics (e.g., venereal disease as a euphemism for sexually transmitted disease), that they become *commonly accepted terms*, or CATs. Additionally, they find that even when annotators agreed on the intended meaning of a euphemism, e.g. *slim* as a euphemism for *skinny*, they still did not agree on the label of euphemistic vs. non euphemistic. The nuance associated with euphemisms still remains one of the biggest challenges.

Felt and Riloff (2020) were one of the first to tackle euphemisms from a computational standpoint. They leverage sentiment analysis to recognize *x-phemisms*, which is the term they use to refer to both euphemisms and dysphemisms. Whereas euphemisms are polite expressions to discuss sensitive topics, dysphemisms are purposely direct, blunt and can be derogatory. They find near-synonym pairs for three topics: lying, firing and stealing, and use a weakly supervised bootstrapping algorithm for semantic lexicon induction (Thelen and Riloff, 2002). They use lexical cues and sentiment analysis to classify phrases as euphemistic, dysphemistic or neutral. Their approach is interesting, as it is the first of its kind and their use of sentiment analysis to identify euphemisms has inspired our work.

Zhu et al. (2021) approach the task of discovering euphemisms from the lens of content moderation. Their goal was the detection of euphemisms used for formal drug names on social media. They define two problems: the first is the detection of euphemisms, and the second is identifying what the euphemisms found actually refer to. However, their view on euphemisms is different from ours, as they treat euphemisms simply as code words. This work is similar to Magu and Luo (2018), who also explore euphemisms as code words in hate speech. Zhu and Bhat (2021) and Zhu et al. (2021) both treat detection and identification as a masked language problem where they use a masked language model (MLM) as a filter to get rid of sentences that are not related to their seedlist of euphemisms and then again to find euphemistic candidates. Like Felt and Riloff (2020), Zhu et al. (2021) and Zhu and Bhat (2021) show promise, though their narrow topic focus limit the kinds of euphemisms that can be found.

Lastly, Kapron-King and Xu (2021) conduct a diachronic evaluation of euphemism usage between genders. While this work is not aimed at finding euphemisms, their work provides many of the PETs used in the creation of the Euphemism Corpus (Gavidia et al., 2022), which we use in this paper.

3 Data

Our work utilizes a Euphemism Corpus created by (Gavidia et al., 2022) as our test data. The raw text data for this corpus comes from The Corpus of Global Web-Based English (GloWbE)(Davies and Fuchs, 2015). GloWbE contains text data for 20 English speaking countries from websites, blogs and forums; this corpus is compiled using just a portion of the US Dialect of English text.
The Euphemism Corpus contains 1,382 euphemistic sentences, each annotated with one potentially euphemistic term per sentence. These potentially euphemistic terms, or PETs (Gavidia et al., 2022) are single and multi word expressions that are used in a euphemistic sense.
Futhermore, we use the US Dialect of English portion of GloWbE to train a Phrases model (gensim) (Rehurek and Sojka, 2011) to create word collocations within our data which are then fed into a word2vec model to produce vector representations for the words in our corpus. The following section explains both of these aspects in further detail.

4 Our Approach

The algorithm developed for this experiment performs the following sub tasks to identify a PET in a sentence: *phrase extraction, phrase filtering, phrase paraphrasing and phrase ranking*. Simply put, the algorithm locates all of the single and multi word expressions within a sentence and through the subsequent tasks, determines which expressions may be a PET.

4.1 Phrase Extraction

We use the phrase (collocation) detection model, Phrases, in the Gensim library (Rehurek and Sojka, 2011) to identify single and multi word expressions within the US Dialect of English portion of GloWbE (Davies and Fuchs, 2015). Phrases takes raw text as input and detects a bigram if a scoring function for two words exceeds a certain threshold. It joins two unigrams into a single token, separated by an underscore. We use Phrases to train our data twice in order to create up to 3 word expressions to account for PETs like *enhanced interrogation techniques*. Upon training, Phrases creates a Phraser object that can be applied to new text data to identify bigram and trigram expressions. As such, we use this Phraser object on the Euphemism Corpus, resulting in identification of single and multiword expressions contained within it.

4.2 Phrase Filtering

The single and multiword expressions found with Phrases now need to be topically filtered. This step is essential in identifying the phrases that are related to a sensitive topic. We remove all stopwords, and then, leveraging the embeddings created with word2vec, calculate the cosine similarity between the phrases and a list of words representing sensitive topics (Gavidia et al., 2022). These sensitive topics include: death, sexual activity, employment, bodily functions, politics, physical/mental attributes, and substances. We notice that many of the PETs in the Euphemism Corpus have a summed cosine similarity score above 1.5; therefore, we empirically set this as the threshold. Every phrase with a similarity measure above this is referred to as a *quality phrase* and moves on to the next task of paraphrasing.

4.3 Phrase Paraphrasing

The idea behind paraphrasing a PET is that, in theory, if we replace quality phrases with "paraphrases" that are more literal, there should be a shift in the sentiment of the sentence. Since using euphemisms can be seen as a conscious lexical choice made to avoid awkward or uncomfortable situations, when we choose to use a PET, our goal is to make our speech less negative, more positive and less offensive. We test this by "paraphrasing" quality phrases using the top 25 most similar words as output by word2vec (excluding paraphrases which contain the quality phrase as a substring, as these are not really distinct alternatives) and perform sentiment analysis to measure negative, positive and offensive scores(Liu et al., 2019) before and after replacement.

Using the distributionally similar words output by word2vec follows the intuition that phrase semantics are determined by their context, and that phrases which have the same mentions should have the same semantics (Li et al., 2022). We recognize that these are not official paraphrases; however, as seen by the example below for the PET *intoxicated*, word2vec produces good results.

```
model.wv.most_similar('intoxicated', topn=10)

[('drunk', 0.7775928378105164),
 ('inebriated', 0.7603026032447815),
 ('drugged', 0.7545843124389648),
 ('assaulted', 0.6952374577522278),
 ('disoriented', 0.6879364252090454),
 ('under_the_influence_of_alcohol', 0.6852758526802063),
 ('hassled', 0.6849539875984192),
 ('stoned', 0.6768251657485962),
 ('tasered', 0.6677494049072266),
 ('accosted', 0.658598005771637)]
```

From this list, we see that "drunk" and "under the influence of alcohol" would be considered literal interpretations of "intoxicated", and as such, would serve as suitable replacements for the paraphrasing task.

4.4 Phrase Ranking

To measure differences in sentiment and offensiveness of the original sentences before and after substituting with alternatives output by word2vec, we use a roBERTa base model trained on tweets for sentiment analysis and offensive language identification (Liu et al., 2019). We chose RoBERTa's sentiment and offensiveness models because they have been shown to be useful in distinguishing PETs from other phrases (Gavidia et al., 2022). The specific scores we utilize are negative, neutral, and positive sentiment scores, as well as non-offensiveness and offensiveness scores. We calculate scores for all replacements and aggregate them into a single score as a measure of which PET had replacements that caused the greatest shift in sentiment. Reasoning that alternatives to PETs are likely more polarized than alternatives to non-PETs, we rank the quality phrases using this aggregate from highest to lowest. The phrases with the top 2 highest scores in each sentence are deemed to be PET candidates.

Empirically, we notice that both offensiveness scores tend to be particularly useful for distinguishing euphemisms from polarized (but otherwise non-euphemistic) terms, so we attribute more weight to them. We hypothesize that both non-offensive and offensive scores are useful because terms that are distributionally similar to PETs are likely to be either (1) similar, non-offensive alternatives or (2) their offensive alternatives. See Appendix A for an illustration of the paraphrasing stage, along with sample sentiment shifts.

5 Results and Discussion

This section provides our quantitative and qualitative analyses and a discussion on the failures and limitations of our algorithm.

5.1 Quantitative Analysis

Table 1 summarizes the results from each step of our procedure. The second column shows the number of total candidate phrases at every stage while the last column shows how many test sentences, out of 1382, still retain the target PETs in the list of candidates at that stage. Note the paraphrasing stage shows no changes as this stage is not meant to reduce the list of PETs.

Stage	# Candidates	# Targets Retained
Phrase Extraction	31348	1251
Phrase Filtering	10503	1198
Phrase Paraphrasing	10503	1198
Phrase Ranking	2728	**725**

Table 1: A summary of the subtasks in our algorithm, along with the number of candidate phrases and PETs that were retained after each.

The algorithm correctly identifies the target PET in 725 sentences. Additionally, through human evaluation, we find that it also identifies new non-target PETs in the data. Out of the 725 PETs deemed to have been successfully detected, 468 of them were ranked as the 1st place candidate, while 257 were 2nd place. Overall, this gives us a success rate of about **52.5%**. Since there was an average of **7.6** phrase candidates per sentence, we calculate the chance of randomly selecting the target to be one of the top two candidates to be $2 * (1/7.6) \approx$ **26.3%**. The sizable improvement over this baseline — which doesn't include new, non-target PETs that were detected — leads us to believe our results are significant.

5.2 Qualitative Analysis

Below, Table 1 includes an example of a correctly identified target PET as well as a new PET that was not annotated for in our test data. While the target PET *mentally disabled* is identified as the second top ranked phrase, we deem the first ranked phrase, *intoxicated person*, to be a PET as well.

We include additional examples of sentences in which the target PET was correctly identified as a top two candidate phrase in Appendix B. Appendix C also showcases more new PETs that were found - by human evaluation. We discuss instances

Sentence: *in addition bats that are found in a room with a person who can not reliably rule out physical contact for example a sleeping person a child a mentally disabled person or an intoxicated person will need to be tested for rabies*
Target PET: mentally disabled
ExtractedPhrases: ['in', 'addition', 'bats', 'that', 'are', 'found', 'in', 'a', 'room', 'with', 'a', 'person_who', 'can_not', 'reliably', 'rule_out', 'physical_contact', 'for', 'example', 'a', 'sleeping', 'person', 'a', 'child', 'a', 'mentally_disabled', 'person', 'or', 'an', 'intoxicated_person', 'will_need', 'to', 'be_tested', 'for', 'rabies']
QualityPhrases: ['bats', 'person_who', 'can_not', 'reliably', 'physical_contact', 'sleeping', 'person', 'child', 'mentally_disabled', 'intoxicated_person', 'be_tested', 'rabies']
RankedPhrases: [('intoxicated person', 2.898948520421982), ('mentally disabled', 2.7745959013700485), ('rabies', 2.036529041826725), ('physical contact', 1.7015496864914894), ('can not', 1.6931570619344711), ('sleeping', 1.267698973417282), ('person', 1.171182319521904), ('person who', 1.0447067320346832), ('bats', 0.9130769670009613), ('be tested', 0.864994041621685), ('reliably', 0.8625116124749184), ('child', 0.23687118291854858)]

Table 2: Example of target PET 'mentally disabled' as second ranked phrase with new PET 'intoxicated person' ranked first.

where our algorithm failed to detect a target PET in the following section.

5.3 Failures

The output candidates may not include the target PET for a couple of reasons: (1) it is not retained from the phrase detection or topic filtering stages, or (2) it produces a low sentiment or offensiveness shift compared to other candidates. Notably, for (1), we notice MWEs are sometimes not collocated properly, either because they aren't detected as a common collocation (e.g., 'between' and 'jobs' are never joined into a single phrase) or because they are collocated with other terms (e.g., 'almost_lost' and 'my_lunch' are detected to be MWEs, but as a result, not 'lost_my_lunch'). For (2), we notice that other candidates (polarized phrases or broad nouns in particular) simply produce higher shifts in all or most sentiment categories compared to the target PET. (See Appendix D for more examples.) As such, while simply computing the increases in sentiment scores and prioritizing offensiveness scores produces workable results for this proof of concept, there is a clear need to experiment with better methods for utilizing sentiment; this is left to future experimentation.

6 Conclusion and Future Work

Our work is a proof of concept for finding PETs in a given euphemistic sentence. While our algorithm produces significant results, we recognize the limitations of our work and propose the following ideas for advancement of this specific task. Firstly, we rely on the Gensim library for identifying multiword expressions and obtaining word embeddings, but experimentation with different parameters and techniques (e.g., using different phrase extraction methods, different bigram scoring functions or contextualized word embeddings) may yield better results. Secondly, a mechanism for filtering each candidate's alternatives could help reduce the number of semantically dissimilar replacements during the paraphrasing stage. Next, while we only use aggregate increases in sentiment and offensiveness scores for ranking candidates, a variety of other methods (e.g., taking averages or maximums) and measures (e.g., indirectness and vagueness) may be useful for distinguishing PETs. Lastly, while the task of differentiating literal versus euphemistic usages of PETs is not a focus on this paper, our algorithm shows some promise on the issue (see Appendix E), and it is an important task that could use future work; Appendix E also shows the performance of our algorithm on unseen data.

Acknowledgements

This material is based upon work supported by the National Science Foundation under Grant No. 1704113.

References

Dildora Oktamovna Bakhriddionova. 2021. The needs of using euphemisms. *Mental Enlightenment Scientific-Methodological Journal*, 2021(06):55–64.

Mark Davies and Robert Fuchs. 2015. Expanding horizons in the study of world englishes with the 1.9 billion word global web-based english corpus (glowbe). *English World-Wide*, 36(1):1–28.

Christian Felt and Ellen Riloff. 2020. Recognizing euphemisms and dysphemisms using sentiment analysis. In *Proceedings of the Second Workshop on Figurative Language Processing*, pages 136–145.

Martha Gavidia, Patrick Lee, Anna Feldman, and Jing Peng. 2022. Cats are fuzzy pets: A corpus and analysis of potentially euphemistic terms. *arXiv preprint arXiv:2205.02728*.

Anna Kapron-King and Yang Xu. 2021. A diachronic evaluation of gender asymmetry in euphemism. In *Proceedings of the 2nd International Workshop on Computational Approaches to Historical Language Change 2021*, pages 28–38, Online. Association for Computational Linguistics.

Savo Karam. 2011. Truths and euphemisms: How euphemisms are used in the political arena. *3L: Language, Linguistics, Literature®*, 17(1).

Jiacheng Li, Jingbo Shang, and Julian McAuley. 2022. Uctopic: Unsupervised contrastive learning for phrase representations and topic mining. *arXiv preprint arXiv:2202.13469*.

Yinhan Liu, Myle Ott, Naman Goyal, Jingfei Du, Mandar Joshi, Danqi Chen, Omer Levy, Mike Lewis, Luke Zettlemoyer, and Veselin Stoyanov. 2019. Roberta: A robustly optimized bert pretraining approach. *arXiv preprint arXiv:1907.11692*.

Rijul Magu and Jiebo Luo. 2018. Determining code words in euphemistic hate speech using word embedding networks. In *Proceedings of the 2nd workshop on abusive language online (ALW2)*, pages 93–100.

Tomas Mikolov, Kai Chen, Greg Corrado, and Jeffrey Dean. 2013. Efficient estimation of word representations in vector space. *arXiv preprint arXiv:1301.3781*.

Hussein Abdo Rababah. 2014. The translatability and use of x-phemism expressions (x-phemization): Euphemisms, dysphemisms and orthophemisms) in the medical discourse. *Studies in Literature and Language*, 9(3):229–240.

Radim Rehurek and Petr Sojka. 2011. Gensim–python framework for vector space modelling. *NLP Centre, Faculty of Informatics, Masaryk University, Brno, Czech Republic*, 3(2).

Michael Thelen and Ellen Riloff. 2002. A bootstrapping method for learning semantic lexicons using extraction pattern contexts. In *Proceedings of the 2002 conference on empirical methods in natural language processing (EMNLP 2002)*, pages 214–221.

Wanzheng Zhu and Suma Bhat. 2021. Euphemistic phrase detection by masked language model. In *Findings of the Association for Computational Linguistics: EMNLP 2021*, pages 163–168, Punta Cana,

Dominican Republic. Association for Computational Linguistics.

Wanzheng Zhu, Hongyu Gong, Rohan Bansal, Zachary Weinberg, Nicolas Christin, Giulia Fanti, and Suma Bhat. 2021. Self-supervised euphemism detection and identification for content moderation. *arXiv preprint arXiv:2103.16808*.

A Example Sentiment Shifts when Replacing PET Candidates

Below we illustrate the paraphrasing stage for two sample PETs (only showing the top 10 replacements for each). Each replacement is listed along with the sentiment shifts it produces in the original sentence (of which, only the increases are aggregated into a final score for the candidate). The five numbers indicate, in order, the [negative, neutral, positive, non-offensive, offensive] sentiment shifts.

Example 1
Original Sentence: the city has told quite a few mistruths in order to get this city office approved **Target PET:** mistruths **Top 10 Replacements:** half-truths [-0.04721798, 0.02886498, 0.018352773, -0.01894176, 0.018941715] outright lies [0.5365411, -0.49552178, -0.041019425, -0.19229656, 0.1922966] falsehoods [0.4495571, -0.4112787, -0.0382785, -0.117421865, 0.11742185] untruths [0.15190402, -0.13002646, -0.021877721, -0.03839171, 0.03839159] half truths [0.12055096, -0.11013514, -0.010415968, -0.029488266, 0.029488236] blatant lies [0.58376455, -0.54074687, -0.04301778, -0.268206, 0.268206] race-baiting [0.08099219, -0.06833702, -0.01265521, -0.05247575, 0.052475646] spewing lies [0.5345895, -0.49333698, -0.041252725, -0.34204996, 0.34205] lies and distortions [0.5648471, -0.5210455, -0.043801878, -0.15087801, 0.15087792] fearmongering [0.12043443, -0.107453406, -0.012981113, -0.029256463, 0.029256403] **Comment:** Note other potentially non-offensive alternatives like "half-truths" and "untruths" (which sometimes result in greater shifts in non-offensiveness than this example), and literal interpretations like "outright lies" and "lies and distortions" (which result in significant offensiveness shifts).

Example 2
Original Sentence: after deadly ethnic riots rocked southern kyrgyzstan last month one georgian minister claimed that russia has been behind the ethnic cleansing of uzbeks **Target PET:** ethnic cleansing **Top 10 Replacements:** genocide [0.022250175, -0.021986336, -0.00026384578, -0.017507195, 0.017507195] collective punishment [-0.027520716, 0.026981518, 0.0005392225, 0.0048098564, -0.004809916] apartheid [-0.00591588, 0.005712375, 0.000203504, 0.011624634, -0.011624634] massacres [0.0055012107, -0.0054178983, -8.32919e-05, -0.004523158, 0.004523158] israeli occupation [-0.019839048, 0.019360632, 0.00047835405, 0.039074123, -0.039074093] islamic terrorism [-0.004287958, 0.0042657405, 2.238946e-05, -0.028740644, 0.028740555] mass murder [0.021661818, -0.021403424, -0.00025822758, -0.08434576, 0.08434579] sectarian conflict [-0.02048409, 0.020332336, 0.00015191245, 0.047309637, -0.047309637] islamization [-0.035422206, 0.03482026, 0.00060210144, 0.027191758, -0.027191669] foreign occupation [-0.018171906, 0.017809838, 0.0003620449, 0.04308176, -0.0430817] **Comment:** Note the literal interpretations "genocide", "massacres" and "mass murder".

B Examples of Successfully Detected PETs

Below are examples where our algorithm successfully detected the target PET. The output is as follows. We identify a Target PET along with the sentence it belongs to. The first set of phrases, *ExtractedPhrases*, are those retrieved through Phrases; after using word2vec to further filter phrases according to our topics, we obtain our *QualityPhrases*; finally, we display our *RankedPhrases* where our candidate PETs appeared in one of the top two rankings.

Example 1
Target PET: psychiatric hospital **Sentence:** *you may believe that if you have signed yourself voluntarily into a psychiatric hospital you can sign yourself out and leave when you decide to do so* **ExtractedPhrases:** ['you_may', 'believe_that', 'if_you', 'have', 'signed', 'yourself', 'voluntarily', 'into', 'a', 'psychiatric_hospital', 'you_can', 'sign', 'yourself', 'out', 'and', 'leave', 'when_you', 'decide', 'to', 'do', 'so'] **QualityPhrases:** ['believe_that', 'if_you', 'voluntarily', 'psychiatric_hospital', 'sign', 'leave', 'when_you', 'decide'] **RankedPhrases:** [('psychiatric hospital', 7.978855848312378), ('voluntarily', 4.409763276576996), ('sign', 2.7386385649442673), ('if you', 2.3423103243112564), ('believe that', 1.915013164281845), ('when you', 1.7038534581661224), ('leave', 1.6538356691598892), ('decide', 1.548440158367157)]

Example 2
Target PET: armed conflict **Sentence:** *when this happens something of considerable legal significance does occur the law of armed conflict begins to govern belligerent relations between the states* **ExtractedPhrases:** ['when', 'this_happens', 'something', 'of', 'considerable', 'legal_significance', 'does_occur', 'the', 'law', 'of', 'armed_conflict', 'begins', 'to', 'govern', 'belligerent', 'relations_between', 'the', 'states'] **QualityPhrases:** ['this_happens', 'considerable', 'legal_significance', 'does_occur', 'law', 'armed_conflict', 'govern', 'belligerent', 'relations_between'] **RankedPhrases:** [('legal significance', 3.8234215676784515), ('armed conflict', 3.674671307206154), ('this happens', 3.6536989957094193), ('belligerent', 2.823164239525795), ('considerable', 1.5059781521558762), ('govern', 1.2904964834451675), ('does occur', 1.1230540722608566), ('relations between', 0.7008794546127319), ('law', 0.5298605561256409)]

Example 3
Target PET: pro-life **Sentence:** *however i am also a person who respects life in all of its forms and so i could also qualify as a pro-life person* **ExtractedPhrases:** ['however_i_am', 'also', 'a', 'person_who', 'respects', 'life', 'in', 'all', 'of', 'its_forms', 'and', 'so', 'i_could', 'also', 'qualify_as', 'a', 'pro-life', 'person'] **QualityPhrases:** ['person_who', 'life', 'its_forms', 'qualify_as', 'pro-life', 'person'] **RankedPhrases:** [('pro-life', 14.923447516746819), ('person', 4.519588744267821), ('qualify as', 2.345528486184776), ('life', 1.7386144306510687), ('its forms', 1.536714962683618), ('person who', 1.4028910771012306)]

C Examples of New PETs Found

Since our algorithm works by placing a candidate PET in one of the top two rankings, we evaluated the results and found that new PETs were found and correctly placed in top ranking positions. One of the limitations of the Euphemism Corpus is that it only includes one annotated PET per sentence, our algorithm shows potential to expand upon the annotations in the corpus to include the new PETs found. We underline the new PETs in the examples below as well as provide our interpretations.

Example 1

Sentence: *or acknowledge real-world trade-offs such as the strong likelihood of amount of of civilian casualties if aq detainees were treated according to either geneva convention or uc criminal law standards*
RankedPhrases: [('civilian casualties', 3.9511645138263702), ('criminal law', 2.082954853773117), ('trade-offs', 2.0316174626350403), ('geneva convention', 1.7544293403625488), ('acknowledge', 1.5634678304195404), ('detainees were', 1.2355359494686127), ('treated', 1.2001541256904602), ('standards', 0.8081734478473663)]
New PET: civilian casualties
Interpretation: the unintended deaths of civilians

Example 2

Sentence: *pelosi says she was briefed by bush administration officials on the legal justification for using waterboarding but that they never followed through on promises to inform her when they actually began using enhanced interrogation techniques*
RankedPhrases: [('using waterboarding', 6.236076384782791), ('enhanced interrogation techniques', 3.640248477458954), ('she was', 1.1687388718128204), ('legal justification', 1.1285315454006195), ('when they', 0.9696991741657257)]
New PET: using waterboarding
Interpretation: a form of torture where a person is strapped down to a board and water is poured over their face in a way that is similar to drowning

Example 3

Sentence: *religious people often complain that secular therapists see their faith as a problem or a symptom rather than as a conviction to be respected and incorporated into the therapeutic dialogue a concern that is especially pronounced among the elderly and twentysomethings*
RankedPhrases: [('secular therapists', 1.9648141264915466), ('especially pronounced', 1.7061323672533035), ('among the elderly', 1.6529535502195358), ('their faith', 1.3943422138690948), ('rather than', 1.2891167849302292), ('concern', 1.2376690953969955), ('religious people', 0.9915256798267365), ('symptom', 0.8965674340724945), ('therapeutic', 0.8766119182109833), ('twentysomethings', 0.8552953451871872), ('be respected', 0.5095183551311493), ('conviction', 0.48858143389225006), ('dialogue', 0.3565850257873535)]
New PET: secular therapists
Interpretation: a non-religious therapist who uses science based therapy methods

D Examples of Failed Target PET Detection

The following examples show instances where our algorithm failed to correctly detect the target PET. We include examples showing sentences in which our MWE extraction method failed to initially recognize a PET as a phrase, and other examples showing where different words, such as action words, had a higher ranking.

Example 1

Target PET: comfort women
Sentence: *and what about the' comfort women industry in israel that uses slavic women as sex slaves*
RankedPhrases: [('sex slaves', 4.3283873945474625), ('slavic', 3.69672554731369), ('women', 1.4681523442268372), ('israel', 1.3728241324424744), ('comfort', 1.0837920159101486), ('industry', 0.8285560309886932)]
Failure: The Target PET 'comfort women' was never identified as a MWE, and thus could not be detected. Additionally, polarized non-euphemisms like "sex slaves" are ranked higher as well as neutral candidates such as "slavic" or "women". This is likely the result of highly polarized alternatives that produce a high score.

Example 2

Target PET: correctional facility
Sentence: *very few correctional facilities have formal vocational education programs that provide offenders with marketable skills and assistance in employment planning*
RankedPhrases:[('offenders', 3.9866801872849464), ('vocational education programs', 2.453631855547428), ('very few', 2.0981270894408226), ('correctional facilities', 1.8522954508662224), ('marketable skills', 1.2003385424613953), ('assistance', 0.7983754873275757), ('employment', 0.5764055326581001), ('formal', 0.4696378782391548)]
Failure: Here, again the Target PET was identified as a phase however the shift in sentiment was greater for the other phrases in the sentence and thus it was not ranked in one of the top two spots.

Example 3

Target PET: pro-life
Sentence: *finally i think many pro-life people are politically naive and are too willing to accept empty promises*
RankedPhrases: [('politically naive', 8.384997591376305), ('empty promises', 4.581491872668266), ('pro-life', 4.001500993967056), ('people', 3.438477225601673), ('i think', 1.7039387673139572)]
Failure: We count this example as a failure as our Target PET is in third place; however, we believe both of the top two candidates to be PETs.
Interpretation: politically naive: someone who has little knowledge and/or experience with politics and empty promises: promises made that are never intended to be carried out

Example 4

Target PET: expecting
Sentence: *i had stopped searching while we were expecting our second child because we were unable to travel if called upon to candidate*
RankedPhrases: [('unable to travel', 7.015634283423424), ('searching', 1.7277799248695374), ('second child', 1.598520651459694), ('candidate', 0.5451297163963318)]
Failure: The target PET is not a phrase candidate because it was incorrectly filtered out at the topic filtering stage. This is likely the case because "expecting" is an otherwise common word.

E New Applications

Below are a few examples where our algorithm shows promise for new applications. We test our algorithm on sentences that are not in our corpus to see if it is able to detect PETs in unseen data. An example is shown below:

Example 1

Sentence: *i heard last week at her birthday party that she has a bun in the oven he whispered as he ate a hot dog bun*
RankedPhrases: [('bun in the oven', 5.764157593250275), ('hot dog bun', 3.9777240827679634), ('he whispered', 3.6007840037345886), ('she has', 2.2385976165533066), ('party', 1.9190692454576492), ('he ate', 1.8731415495276451), ('her birthday', 1.3221752345561981)]
New PET: bun in the oven
Interpretation: a baby in a belly; a pregnancy

Below, we show an example where our algorithm shows potential in distinguishing euphemistic versus non-euphemistic usages of the same word. First, we show the output for a non-euphemistic sentence containing a non-euphemistic usage of the PET *dismissed*:

Example 2

Sentence: *the class is dismissed and we bow to each other expressing our gratitude for the shared experience*
RankedPhrases: [('shared experience', 3.9033331400714815), ('bow', 3.663858987390995), ('each other', 2.1924624936655164), ('dismissed', 1.9963299129158258), ('expressing', 1.848377185408026), ('class', 0.9816022356972098)]
Interpretation: allowed to leave or disband

Now, we show the output for a sentence containing a euphemistic usage of *dismissed*. Note how *dismissed* is now detected as a euphemism, as well as its higher sentiment score compared to the previous example.

Example 3

Sentence: *at nichols college outside worcester massachusetts a non-tenured professor who questioned the leadership of the college president was summarily dismissed*
RankedPhrases: [('dismissed', 5.921802910044789), ('was summarily', 3.158419349696487), ('worcester massachusetts', 1.4444764871150255), ('college', 1.196013430133462), ('non-tenured', 1.1229130360297859), ('president', 1.0259317518211901), ('leadership', 1.0157726714387536)]
Interpretation: forced to leave a position; fired

Author Index